WITHDRAWN

Pulitzer Prize Editorials
America's Best Editorial Writing, 1917–1979

Pulitzer Prize Editorials
America's Best Editorial Writing, 1917–1979

W. DAVID SLOAN

Iowa State University Press / AMES

1 9 8 0

W. David Sloan is assistant professor of journalism at the University of Arkansas and is owner, columnist, and editorial writer of the *Farmington* (Ark.) *Mercury,* a weekly newspaper.

ACKNOWLEDGMENTS

We gratefully acknowledge the permissions granted to reprint material appearing first in the following publications:

1917—Frank H. Simonds, in the *New York Tribune;* 1918—Henry Watterson, in the *Louisville Courier-Journal;* 1920—Harvey E. Newbranch, in the *Omaha Evening World-Herald;* 1922—Frank M. O'Brien, in the *New York Herald;* 1923—William Allen White, in the *Emporia Gazette;* 1924—Frank Buxton, in the *Boston Herald;* 1925—Robert Lathan, in the *Charleston News & Courier;* 1926—Edward M. Kingsbury, in the *New York Times,* © 1926-1954 by The New York Times Co.; 1927—F. Lauriston Bullard, in the *Boston Herald;* 1928—Grover Cleveland Hall, in the *Montgomery Advertiser;* 1929—Louis Isaac Jaffe, in the *Norfolk Virginian-Pilot;* 1931—Charles S. Ryckman, in the *Fremont Tribune;* 1933, 1944—Henry J. Haskell, in the *Kansas City Star;* 1934—Edwin P. Chase, in the *Atlantic News-Telegraph;* 1936—Felix Morley, in the *Washington Post,* and George B. Parker, Scripps-Howard Newspapers; 1937—John W. Owens, in the *Baltimore Sun;* 1938—William Wesley Waymack, in the *Des Moines Register and Tribune,* © 1936, Des Moines Register and Tribune Co.; 1939—Ronald G. Callvert, in the *Portland Oregonian;* 1940—Bart Howard, in the *St. Louis Post-Dispatch;* 1941—Reuben Maury, in the *New York Daily News,* © 1941 News Syndicate Co., Inc.; 1942—Geoffrey Parsons, in the *New York Herald Tribune;* 1943—Forrest W. Seymour, in the *Des Moines Register and Tribune,* © 1942, Des Moines Register and Tribune Co.; 1945—George W. Potter, in the *Providence Journal-Bulletin;* 1946—Hodding Carter, in the *Delta Democrat-Times;* 1947—William H. Grimes, in the *Wall Street Journal,* © Dow Jones & Co.; 1948—Virginius Dabney, in the *Richmond Times-Dispatch;* 1949—John H. Crider, in the *Boston Herald,* and Herbert Elliston, in the *Washington Post;* 1950—Carl M. Saunders, in the *Jackson Citizen Patriot;* 1951—William H. Fitzpatrick, in the *New Orleans States;* 1952—Louis LaCoss, in the *St. Louis Globe-Democrat;* 1953—Vermont Connecticut Royster, in the *Wall Street Journal,* © Dow Jones & Co.; 1954—Don Murray, in the *Boston Herald;* 1955—Royce Howes, in the *Detroit Free Press;* 1956—Lauren K. Soth, in the *Des Moines Register and Tribune,* © 1955, Des Moines Register and Tribune Co.; 1957—Buford Boone, in the *Tuscaloosa News;* 1958—Harry S. Ashmore, in the *Arkansas Gazette;* 1959—Ralph McGill, in the *Atlanta Constitution;* 1960—Lenoir Chambers, in the *Norfolk Virginian-Pilot;* 1961—William J. Dorvillier, in the *San Juan Star;* 1962—Thomas M. Storke, in the *Santa Barbara News-Press;* 1963—Ira B. Harkey, Jr., in the *Pascagoula Chronicle;* 1964—Hazel Brannon Smith, in the *Lexington Advertiser* and *Durant News;* 1965—John R. Harrison, in the *Gainesville Sun;* 1966—Robert Lasch, in the *St. Louis Post-Dispatch;* 1967—Eugene Patterson, in the *Atlanta Constitution;* 1968—John S. Knight, in the Knight Newspapers; 1969—Paul Greenberg, in the *Pine Bluff Commercial;* 1970—Philip L. Geyelin, in the *Washington Post;* 1971—Horance G. Davis, Jr., in the *Gainesville Sun;* 1972—John Strohmeyer, in the *Bethlehem Globe-Times;* 1973—Roger B. Linscott, in the *Berkshire Eagle;* 1974—F. Gilman Spencer, in the *Trentonian;* 1975—John Daniell Maurice, in the *Charleston Daily Mail;* 1976—Philip P. Kerby, in the *Los Angeles Times,* © 1975, *Los Angeles Times;* 1977—Foster Church, Norman F. Cardoza, and Warren L. Lerude, in the *Nevada State Journal* and the *Reno Evening Gazette;* 1978—Meg Greenfield, in the *Washington Post;* and 1979—Ed Yoder, in the *Washington Star.*

First edition, 1980

Library of Congress Cataloging in Publication Data

Main entry under title:

Pulitzer prize editorials.

1. Editorials. 2. Pulitzer prizes. I. Sloan, William David, 1947–
PN4726.P8   081   80–11689
ISBN 0–8138–1490–1

CONTENTS

PREFACE

A WORK of the nature of this anthology would be close to impossible without the help of numerous individuals. I am grateful to the following for the time and consideration they gave. Pulitzer Prize winners who assisted, always kindly, include J. D. Maurice, Warren L. Lerude, Paul Greenberg, John S. Knight, Virginius Dabney, Hazel Brannon Smith, John Strohmeyer, William Dorvillier, Ed Yoder, and Meg Greenfield.

Others who provided editorials or information, often only after time-consuming efforts of searching old newspaper files and corresponding with other sources, were Edward G. Hawkins, editor of the editorial page, *The Trentonian* (Trenton, N. J.); F. T. Weaver, manager, *Jackson* (Mich.) *Citizen Patriot;* Joseph R. L. Sterne, editor of the editorial pages, *Baltimore Sun;* Anthony Day, editor of the the editorial pages, *Los Angeles Times;* Joe H. Stroud, editor, *Detroit Free Press;* John Springer, librarian, *Kansas City* (Mo.) *Star and Times;* Don Benson, director of public events, *Des Moines Register and Tribune;* James B. Boone, Jr., president, *Tuscaloosa* (Ala.) *News;* Harry W. Baehr, former editorial writer, *New York Herald Tribune;* James H. Wagner of the Scripps-Howard Newspapers; Hal Gulliver, editor, *Atlanta Constitution;* Kevin Parrish, managing editor, *Fremont* (Neb.) *Tribune;* John Ball, executive editor, *Santa Barbara* (Calif.) *News-Press;* Ray Jenkins, editor, *Montgomery Advertiser* and *Alabama Journal;* Charles Scarritt, retired professor of journalism, University of Alabama; Edward Grimsley, editor of the editorial page, *Richmond* (Va.) *Times-Dispatch;* John H. Metcalfe, assistant to the editor, *New York Daily News;* John O. Wynne, vice-president, Landmark Communications, Inc.; William F. Woo, editor of the editorial page, *St. Louis Post-Dispatch;* Martin L. Duggan, editorial page editor, *St. Louis Globe-Democrat;* and Walter G. Cowan, editor, *New Orleans States-Item.* Of special help at the Pulitzer Prize administrator's office at Columbia University were Richard T. Baker, Rose Valenstein, and Robin Kuzen.

Permission to reprint editorials in this anthology has been given by the following institutions and individuals: *International Herald Tribune; Louisville Courier-Journal; Omaha* (Neb.) *Evening World-Herald;* Mrs. William L. (Katharine) White, *Emporia* (Kan.) *Gazette; Boston Herald; Charleston* (S.C.) *News & Courier; New York Times; Montgomery Advertiser* and *Alabama Journal;* Landmark Communications, Inc. (owner of the *Norfolk Virginian-Pilot*); *Fremont* (Neb.) *Tribune; Kansas City Star and Times; Atlantic* (Iowa) *News-Telegraph; Washington Post;* Scripps-Howard Newspapers; *Baltimore Sun; Des Moines Register and Tribune; Portland Oregonian; St. Louis Post-Dispatch; New York Daily News; Providence* (R. I.) *Journal-Bulletin; Greenville* (Miss.) *Delta Democrat Times; Wall Street Journal;* Virginius Dabney, *Richmond* (Va.) *Times-Dispatch; Jackson* (Mich.) *Citizen Patriot;* The Times-Picayune Publishing Co.; *St. Louis Globe-Democrat; Detroit Free Press; Tuscaloosa* (Ala.) *News; Arkansas Gazette; Atlanta Constitution;* William J. Dorvillier and *San Juan* (Puerto Rico) *Star; Santa Barbara* (Calif.) *News-Press;* Hazel Brannon Smith, *Lexington* (Miss.) *Advertiser; Gainesville* (Fla.) *Daily Sun;* John S. Knight, Knight Newspapers; Paul Greenberg, *Pine Bluff* (Ark.) *Commercial;* John Strohmeyer, *Bethlehem* (Pa.) *Globe-Times; The Trentonian* (Trenton, N. J.); J. D. Maurice, *Charleston* (W.Va.) *Daily Mail; Los Angeles Times;* Warren Lerude, *Nevada State Journal* and *Reno Evening Gazette;* and Ed Yoder, *Washington Star.*

W. DAVID SLOAN

The Pulitzer Prize for Editorial Writing

JOSEPH PULITZER'S chief concern in his *New York World* centered on its editorial page. It was to be expected, then, that his will establishing awards for journalism and letters included a prize for "the best editorial article written during the previous year." In setting out his plans for a journalism school at Columbia University, Pulitzer in 1902 had indicated strongly that he wished "the College to pay from the large income I am providing, a sum of ——— in annual prizes to particular journalists or writers for various accomplishments. For instance, they might offer an annual prize of one thousand dollars for the best editorial." Since its inauguration in 1917, the Pulitzer Prize has become recognized as journalism's highest award for editorial writing.

Yet, no collection of winning editorials exists except in the archives of the Pulitzer Prize administration at Columbia University. It is inaccessible to most people. Many newspapers do not have their winning editorials on file. Rarely have any of the editorials been reprinted or made available to journalists and students of editorial writing. This is an odd situation for what are usually considered ideal models of editorial writing. To remedy this problem is the purpose of this anthology.

The original description of the editorial-writing award was as follows: "For distinguished editorial writing in a United States newspaper, published daily, Sunday, or at least once a week, during the year, the test of excellence being clearness of style, moral purpose, sound reasoning, and power to influence public opinion in the right direction." A number of rule changes and additions have been made since 1917.

In 1928 the last phrase was changed to "power to influence public opinion in what the writer conceives to be the right direction."

While Pulitzer had indicated a desire to have the award based on the best individual editorial during a year, the emphasis is now placed on "the whole volume of the writer's editorial work during the year." Until 1933, every award except one—Grover Cleveland Hall's in 1928—was based on an individual editorial. Since then the award has been given only three times for a single editorial, although during a number of years a particular editorial has been cited as exemplary of a writer's work.

When the award was based on individual editorials, there was little problem with limits on the number of editorials a writer could enter in the contest. However, when Don Murray of the *Boston Herald* submitted more than 100 for his 1954 exhibit, the Pulitzer personnel decided it was time for a crackdown. After that, exhibits were to include no more than 12 editorials, though in unusual circumstances more would be acceptable. In practice, the limit has not been strictly observed. Today, 20 editorials are considered the maximum.

One other rule change has probably been of some practical interest to winners. In 1953 the original $500 prize was increased to $1,000.

Members of the public sometimes think that every editorial written in a year in the United States is considered for the Pulitzer Prize. The Pulitzer for editorial writing, however, is like most other journalism awards. The author—or someone acting in the author's behalf—must apply for it. The deadline for entries, known as "exhibits," is February 1. Though procedures have varied over the years, at present the exhibits are reviewed by a 5-member jury of journalism professionals. Their suggestions are passed on to a 15-member board (with 13 voting members), which makes the final decision of who will receive the prize. The winner is announced in the spring, usually in April.

Until the mid-1970s an Advisory Board reviewed the nominations made by the jurors and sent its suggestions to the Columbia University trustees. The trustees then decided who would receive the prize, the winner normally being the one suggested by the board. The trustees' involvement with the award was discontinued in the middle of the 1970s and the final decision left to the board. Despite the change, the name Advisory Board was retained until 1979. Changes in terminology had been contemplated for some time, and controversies over the 1978 award spurred action. The jurors who submit nominations for winner are now designated the nominating jurors. The Advisory Board, which decides who wins the award, became The Pulitzer Prize Board. One reason for the change was to indicate that jury nominations are only recommendations to the board and are not binding.

Another change requires the jury to make from three to five nominations or to recommend that no one be awarded the prize. In years past it could propose that either one entry or several entries or no entry at all was worthy. The jury is also now required to list its recommendations in alphabetical order rather than in order of preference, although the jury does have the option of submitting a special recommendation to the board in a separate statement.

In most years, the winner of the Pulitzer Prize has been the writer preferred by the jury, but this has not always been the case. In 1978, for example, the Pulitzer Prize Board (then Advisory Board) chose Meg Greenfield of the *Washington Post* over Paul Greenberg of the *Pine Bluff*

(Ark.) *Commercial,* whom the jury had recommended. In 1979, the jury's choice of Philip Goldsmith of the *Philadelphia Inquirer* was bypassed in favor of Edwin Yoder of the *Washington Star.*

One recipient of the award is normally chosen, though there are exceptions. Twice, in 1936 and 1949, two winners were named. On five occasions no award for editorial writing was given. The omissions met with wide criticism, and an award has been made every year since 1935. Besides the years when the award was withheld, there are two years from which no records of winning editorials are available. Files in the Pulitzer Prize office do not include the exhibit of George B. Parker (1936), and Scripps-Howard Newspapers has not kept a file of his entry. Virginius Dabney of the *Richmond* (Va.) *Times-Dispatch* received the 1948 award without submitting an entry. For this anthology, I have pieced together parts of an editorial thought to have been included in Parker's entry and have included a Dabney editorial for which he won the 1948 Sigma Delta Chi editorial-writing award.

I would like to be able to say that all the Pulitzer Prize editorials are outstanding, but in all honesty they are not. The most obvious characteristic of many is their ordinariness. The cause of this problem lies at least in part with the selection process for the prize. Only a small number of editorials written during a year are considered. Obviously it would be impossible for judges to read every editorial written in the nation during a year. Thus, only editorials submitted as official entries are considered. And only a relatively small number of exhibits, about 60 a year, are submitted—probably because of lack of interest by newspapers in the awards, lack of knowledge about the entry process, and the amount of work involved in preparing an exhibit. Whatever the reason, the fact is that editorials from only a relative handful of newspapers are considered by judges.

The qualifications of judges may also sometimes contribute to the quality of winning editorials. There is no reason to believe that Pulitzer judges are either extraordinarily qualified to determine editorial perfection or omniscient. Judges usually are respected editorial writers, but nothing makes Pulitzer judges more qualified than judges of several other editorial-writing contests.

The judges are also humans, and as humans have their peculiar outlooks and biases. One obvious area in which judges' attitudes appear is subject matter of winning editorials. A typical subject has been press freedom. At least five winning writers have dealt either solely or primarily with the topic, a reflection of the egocentric interests of journalists and Pulitzer judges. Another popular topic has been race relations, treated with a strong emphasis on the rule of law. The first winning editorial on the subject was Harvey Newbranch's "Law and the Jungle" of 1920. Several later winners have duplicated Newbranch's approach, but none has done a better job. One suspects that all an editorial writer would have had to do to win the Pulitzer in the late 1950s and much of the 1960s would have been to be fortunate enough to live in a southern town having racial difficulties and write editorials calling for obedience to the U.S. Constitution. Winning editorials also have exhibited similar political leanings during specific periods. Every winning editorial writer through 1956 who covered a political or economic topic (unless we consider F. Lauriston Bullard's 1927 winner, "We Submit," a political editorial) exhibited conservative or even reactionary tendencies, usually siding with the Republican party. Strong nationalism or patriotism was also a hallmark of many winners. In the late 1950s a shift took place. Editorials since then have been marked by liberalism, strongly supporting civil rights and liberties in the face of prevalent social or governmental attitudes. The change in contest rules on "power to influence public opinion in what the writer conceives to be the right direction" has been meaningless. The judges' conception of what is the right direction apparently still governs. For example, a writer who takes a highly unpopular stand such as support of discrimination in race relations or opposition to freedom of the press will not be likely to win the Pulitzer in the near future.

Routineness of winning editorials probably has been encouraged also by the change from selecting a single outstanding editorial to basing the prize on a large volume of editorials by the writer. So a writer today who pens one "great" editorial along with standard fare may have little chance. What we get from winners is usually a collection of editorials above average in quality but not classic in perfection. The Pulitzer administration could consider giving two awards: one (as is now done) for a writer's volume of editorials and another for an individual editorial.

Though most recent winning editorials have been of acceptable quality, a large number of them seem to have at least one of two common problems: dullness of writing and lack of unity. Dullness seems much more prevalent today than in the early years of the award. Compare, for example, the style and tone of such editorials as "Vae Victis!" (1918), "The Unknown Soldier" (1922), "The House of a Hundred Sorrows" (1926), and "The Gentleman from Nebraska" (1931) with most of the editorials in, say, the 1970s. A distinct difference in phrasing, feeling, and flavor can be noted. This is not to say that no recent editorials are interestingly written. F. Gilman Spencer, for example, winner of the 1974 award, certainly has a distinctive style. The change in style is not an indication of a change in writing ability. It more accurately reflects a changing concept of what an editorial should do and be. Earlier editorials often relied on the writer's personality and on formal logic to persuade readers; today the editorial more often bases its attempt to persuade, if indeed it even has persuasion as its purpose, on statement of fact and an apparent unbiased analysis. Its writing style, then, is what we might call "plain English," intended primarily to communicate and divorced from any other purpose. While early writers tried to be aesthetic, recent writers more often try simply to be informative.

Breakdown of unity in editorials is as common as dull style. Usually this results when the writer has had no clear thematic focus or structural design to the editorial or has attempted to bring in too many aspects or details in too short a space. This problem is apparent in a number of editorials in this anthology.

Despite these shortcomings, editorials that have won the Pulitzer Prize are probably the best sources of illustrations of editorial quality. The large number of editorial winners over such a span of years offer examples of almost all aspects of editorial writing, from subject matter to style to analysis to interpretation to argumentation.

A few things should be said about how the editorials in this anthology were selected. In the years in which the Pulitzer was given for a single editorial, obviously that editorial is included. For most other years, only one editorial from the winning exhibit is included. In any year in which the Pulitzer committees cited a specific editorial from the winning exhibit (such as 1939 and 1946), that editorial is used in this anthology. When no specific editorial was cited, I have chosen an editorial that either seems outstanding or has been frequently cited by other writers. When no editorial stands out from the rest in the exhibit, I have chosen an editorial that seems typical of the work of the winning writer.

Following is a list of winners of the Pulitzer Prize for Editorial Writing and official citations made by the Columbia University Board of Trustees. A number of errors, primarily in phrasing of editorial titles, have been made in the official citations. Such errors have been corrected in the list here, accounting for differences some readers might notice between this and the citations maintained by the Pulitzer Prize office.

1917 *NEW YORK TRIBUNE* for an editorial article on the first anniversary of the sinking of the *Lusitania.*

1918 *LOUISVILLE COURIER-JOURNAL* for the editorial article "Vae Victis!" and the editorial "War Has Its Compensations."

1919 No award.

1920 HARVEY E. NEWBRANCH, *Omaha Evening World-Herald,* for an editorial entitled "Law and the Jungle."

1921 No award.

1922 FRANK M. O'BRIEN, *New York Herald,* for an article entitled "The Unknown Soldier."

1923 WILLIAM ALLEN WHITE, *Emporia* (Kan.) *Gazette,* for an editorial entitled "To an Anxious Friend."

1924 *BOSTON HERALD* for an editorial entitled "Who Made

Coolidge?'' A special prize of $1,000 was awarded to the widow of the late FRANK I. COBB, *New York World,* in recognition of the distinction of her husband's editorial writing and service.

1925 *CHARLESTON* (S.C.) *NEWS & COURIER* for the editorial entitled "The Plight of the South."

1926 *NEW YORK TIMES,* by Edward M. Kingsbury, for the editorial entitled "The House of a Hundred Sorrows."

1927 *BOSTON HERALD,* by F. Lauriston Bullard, for the editorial entitled "We Submit."

1928 GROVER CLEVELAND HALL, *Montgomery* (Ala.) *Advertiser,* for his editorials against gangsterism, floggings and racial and religious intolerance.

1929 LOUIS ISAAC JAFFE, *Norfolk Virginian-Pilot,* for his editorial entitled "An Unspeakable Act of Savagery," which is typical of a series of articles written on the lynching evil and in successful advocacy of legislation to prevent it.

1930 No award.

1931 CHARLES S. RYCKMAN, *Fremont* (Neb.) *Tribune,* for the editorial entitled "The Gentleman from Nebraska."

1932 No award.

1933 *KANSAS CITY* (MO.) *STAR* for its series of editorials on national and international topics.

1934 EDWIN P. CHASE, *Atlantic* (Iowa) *News-Telegraph,* for an editorial entitled "Where Is Our Money?"

1935 No award.

1936 FELIX MORLEY, *Washington Post,* and GEORGE B. PARKER, Scripps-Howard Newspapers, for distinguished editorial writing during the year.

1937 JOHN W. OWENS, *Baltimore Sun,* for distinguished editorial writing during the year.

1938 WILLIAM WESLEY WAYMACK, *Des Moines Register and Tribune,* for his distinguished editorial writing during the year.

1939 RONALD G. CALLVERT, *Portland Oregonian,* for his distinguished editorial writing during the year, as exemplified by the editorial entitled "My Country 'Tis of Thee."

1940 BART HOWARD, *St. Louis Post-Dispatch,* for his distinguished editorial writing during the year.

1941 REUBEN MAURY, *New York Daily News,* for his distinguished editorial writing during the year.

1942 GEOFFREY PARSONS, *New York Herald Tribune,* for his distinguished editorial writing during the year.

1943 FORREST W. SEYMOUR, *Des Moines Register and Tribune,* for his editorials published during the calendar year 1942.

1944 *KANSAS CITY* (MO.) *STAR,* by Henry J. Haskell, for editorials written during the calendar year 1943.

1945 GEORGE W. POTTER, *Providence Journal-Bulletin,* for his editorials published during the calendar year 1944, especially for his editorials on the subject of freedom of the press.

1946 HODDING CARTER, *Delta Democrat-Times* (Greenville, Miss.), for a group of editorials published during the year 1945 on the subject of racial, religious and economic intolerance, as exemplified by the editorial "Go For Broke."

1947 WILLIAM H. GRIMES, *Wall Street Journal,* for distinguished editorial writing during the year.

1948 VIRGINIUS DABNEY, *Richmond Times-Dispatch,* for distinguished editorial writing during the year.

1949 JOHN H. CRIDER, *Boston Herald,* and HERBERT ELLISTON, *Washington Post,* for distinguished editorial writing during the year.

1950 CARL M. SAUNDERS, *Jackson* (Mich.) *Citizen Patriot,* for distinguished editorial writing during the year.

1951 WILLIAM HARRY FITZPATRICK, *New Orleans States,* for his series of editorials analyzing and clarifying a very important constitutional issue, which is described by the general heading of the series, "Government by Treaty."

1952 LOUIS LaCOSS, *St. Louis Globe-Democrat,* for his editorial entitled "The Low Estate of Public Morals."

1953 VERMONT CONNECTICUT ROYSTER, *Wall Street Journal,* for distinguished editorial writing during the year.

1954 *BOSTON HERALD,* for a series of editorials by Don Murray, on the "New Look" in national defense, that won wide attention for their analysis of changes in American military policy.

1955 *DETROIT FREE PRESS,* for an editorial by Royce Howes, on the cause of a strike, impartially and clearly analyzing the responsibility of both labor and management for a local union's unauthorized strike in July, 1954, that rendered 45,000 Chrysler Corporation workers idle and unpaid. By pointing out how and why the parent united automobile workers' union ordered the local strike called off and stating that management let dissatisfaction get out of hand, the editorial made a notable contribution to public understanding of the whole program of the respective responsibilities and relationships of labor and management in the field.

1956 LAUREN K. SOTH, *Des Moines Register and Tribune,* for the editorial inviting a farm delegation from the Soviet Union to visit Iowa, which led directly to the Russian farm visit to the United States.

1957 BUFORD BOONE, *Tuscaloosa* (Ala.) *News,* for his fearless and reasoned editorials in a community inflamed by a segregation issue, an outstanding example of his work being the editorial entitled "What a Price for Peace," published on February 7, 1956.

1958   HARRY S. ASHMORE, executive editor of the *Arkansas Gazette,* for the forcefulness, dispassionate analysis and clarity of his editorials on the school integration conflict in Little Rock.

1959   RALPH McGILL, editor of the *Atlanta Constitution,* for distinguished editorial writing during 1958, as exemplified in his editorial "A Church, A School—," and for his long, courageous and effective editorial leadership.

1960   LENOIR CHAMBERS, editor of the *Norfolk Virginian-Pilot,* for his series of editorials on the school segregation problem in Virginia, as exemplified by "The Year Virginia Closed the Schools," published January 1, 1959, and "The Year Virginia Opened the Schools," published December 31, 1959.

1961   WILLIAM J. DORVILLIER, *San Juan* (Puerto Rico) *Star,* for his editorials on clerical interference in the 1960 gubernatorial election in Puerto Rico.

1962   THOMAS M. STORKE of the *Santa Barbara* (Calif.) *News-Press* for his forceful editorials calling public attention to the activities of a semisecret organization known as the John Birch Society.

1963   IRA B. HARKEY, JR., editor and publisher of the *Pascagoula* (Miss.) *Chronicle,* for his courageous editorials devoted to the processes of law and reason during the integration crisis in Mississippi in 1962.

1964   HAZEL BRANNON SMITH of the *Lexington* (Miss.) *Advertiser* for steadfast adherence to her editorial duty in the face of great pressure and opposition.

1965   JOHN R. HARRISON of the *Gainesville* (Fla.) *Sun* for his successful editorial campaign for better housing in his city.

1966   ROBERT LASCH of the *St. Louis Post-Dispatch* for his distinguished editorial writing in 1965.

1967   EUGENE C. PATTERSON of the *Atlanta Constitution* for his editorials during the year.

1968   JOHN S. KNIGHT of the Knight Newspapers for distinguished editorial writing.

1969   PAUL GREENBERG of the *Pine Bluff* (Ark.) *Commercial* for his editorials during 1968.

1970   PHILIP L. GEYELIN, *Washington Post,* for his editorials during 1969.

1971   HORANCE G. DAVIS, JR., of the *Gainesville* (Fla.) *Sun* for his editorials in support of the peaceful desegregation of Florida's schools.

1972   JOHN STROHMEYER of the *Bethlehem* (Pa.) *Globe-Times* for his editorials during 1972.

1973   ROGER B. LINSCOTT of the *Berkshire Eagle* (Pittsfield, Mass.) for his editorials during 1972.

Pulitzer Prize Editorials
America's Best Editorial Writing, 1917–1979

The Lusitania *Anniversary*

(MAY 7, 1916)

F R A N K   H.   S I M O N D S
New York Tribune

UNTIL the sinking of the ship *Lusitania* on May 7, 1915, Americans were widely split and many were truly neutral toward the contestants in World War I. But a turning point in public opinion came with the sinking. This was the opinion of many historians, including Frank Simonds, editor of the *New York Tribune*. In a multivolume history of World War I published in 1919, Simonds says that with the sinking, Americans began to see the true, inhumane nature of Germany. Yet at the time of the *Lusitania* tragedy, fewer than half a dozen American papers asked for war. One of those that did was Simonds's *Tribune*. In a show of militant patriotism, it warned that "the nation which remembered the sailors of the Maine will not forget the civilians of the *Lusitania*." On the first anniversary of the sinking, Simonds wrote the editorial that won the first Pulitzer Prize. It is an attempt to characterize the European war as one between civilization and barbarism. Though today it may appear extremely simplistic, it did mirror Simonds's true opinion and was not simply an artificial attempt to appeal to his readers' baser natures. In 1916 the editorial, despite its simplicity, was effective propaganda considering the frame of mind of Americans.

ON the anniversary of the sinking of the *Lusitania* it is natural and fitting that Americans should review all that has happened since a wanton murder first brought to this side of the Atlantic a nascent realization of the issue that was being decided on a world battlefield.

There will be no anger and no passion in American minds. We have never asked, never desired, that the slaughter should be avenged. No portion of the American people or of the American press has clamored for vengeance, no man or political party has demanded that there should be German lives taken because American lives had been ended.

It is not too difficult to reconstitute our own minds as we stood in the presence of that supreme atrocity. The horror that seized a whole nation in that moment has no counterpart in our history. We have known war, we have fought Great Britain twice, we have fought Spain and Mexico; within our own boundaries we have conducted the most desperate civil war in human history.

But it was not the emotion provoked by war or the acts of war which moved Americans. It was not even the emotion stirred by the sinking of the *Maine* nearly two decades ago. It was certainly something utterly remote from the feelings of our fathers and grandfathers on the morrow of the firing on Fort Sumter.

The *Lusitania* Massacre was not an act of war. The victims were not soldiers, only a portion of them were men. Essentially the thing was a new phenomenon to the American people. It was at first incomprehensible, unbelievable. Despite the solid and inescapable evidences of death, men's intelligence doubted what their senses told them.

So for days and weeks the American people stood doubtful and puzzled. They waited for that evidence they expected, they believed would come; that there had been an accident, a mistake, the blunder of a subordinate which would be repudiated by a government, the crime of a navy which would be disavowed by a people. But instead far borne across the seas they heard the songs of triumph of thousands of German men and women, who hailed the crime as a victory, the eternal disgrace as an everlasting honor.

Day by day, week by week, we Americans have since then been learning that we are not in the presence of a war between nations, a conflict between rival powers; that we are not the agonized witnesses of one more conflagration provoked by conflicting ambitions of hereditary enemies. We have been learning that what is going forward remorselessly, steadily, is a war between civilization and barbarism, between humanity and savagery; between the light of modern times and the darkness of the years that followed the collapse of Rome.

Time and again Americans have been murdered, time and again our government, our people, have had recourse to the ordinary machinery and the ordinary conceptions of civilized life. But each time we have beheld the utter collapse of every appeal based upon reason, justice, common humanity. The Germans who slew our women and our children flung us back the challenge that they and not we possessed the true civilization, and that their civilization, their Kultur, was expressed in their works, which were altogether good and right.

Slowly, steadily, we have been learning. We still have much to learn, but the primary truth is coming home to many day by day. This German phenomenon which fills the world is a new thing and an old thing; it is new in our generation, it is new in recent centuries; but it is as old as that other barbarism which, descending upon the Roman civilization, beat upon it and spread destruction until it was conquered and tamed amidst the ruins and the desert it had created.

The French, who see things as they are, have beheld and appraised the German phenomenon justly. The British, like ourselves, have partially and temporarily failed to understand the nature of the German assault. We have insisted upon applying to the German mind our own standards and upon believing that the Germans thought as we thought, believed as we believed, but were temporarily and terribly betrayed by a military spirit and by dynastic madness.

Nothing is less true, nothing more fatal to a just appreciation of the essential fact in the world in which we live. These things which we name crimes are neither accidents nor excesses; they are not regretted or condemned by a majority or even a minority of the German people. They are accepted by Kaiser and peasant; they are practised by Crown Prince and private soldier; they are a portion of what Germany holds to be her right and her mission.

The *Lusitania* Massacre should have been a final illumination for us. Blazing up as it did, it should have revealed to us the ashes of Belgium and the ruins of Northern France. We should have seen in our slain women and children the sisters and fellows in misfortune of those who died more shamefully in Louvain and a score more of Belgian cities. We should have seen the German idea working here and revealing in each incident the same handiwork, the same detail. All these things were similar as the different impressions left by a single stamp.

We did not see. We have not yet as a nation, or as a people, perceived that the German phenomenon is an attack upon civilization by barbarism, a barbarism which combines the science of the laboratory with the savagery of the jungle, but a barbarism because it denies all those doctrines and principles which have been accepted after long years as the proof of human progress and the glory of mankind's advance.

In France the people will show you the atrocities of Germany committed not upon human beings, but upon the inanimate things, the destruction of the village church and the Rheims Cathedral, of the little thing of beauty quite as well as the larger and more famous thing, with far more emphasis than they will recount the horrors suffered by women and children. In the assault upon things beautiful because they are beautiful, an assault provoked neither by lust nor by passion, they recognize the revelation of that which is essential barbarism.

For us the *Lusitania* Massacre was a beginning. It was only a beginning, but it was not possible then, it is hardly possible now, for men and women, living in peace, under the protection of laws framed to protect human liberty and human rights, living in the full sunlight of this Twentieth Century, to believe that suddenly there has broken out from the depths the frightful and the all-destroying spirit of eras long forgotten.

We have been learning—we must continue to learn. The road of suffering and humiliation is still long. But the *Lusitania* was a landmark and it will endure in American history. Our children and our children's children recalling this anniversary will think of it as did the Romans over long generations, after the first inroads of the barbarians had reached their walls.

Today is not a day for anger or passion. It is not in anger or in passion that civilized men go forth to deal with wild animals, to abolish the peril which comes from the jungle or out of the darkness. We do not hate Germans and we shall not hate Germans because on this day a year ago American men, women and children were slain wilfully, wantonly, to serve a German end, slain without regard to sex or condition, slain in the broad daylight by German naval officers and men whose countrymen hailed the killing as the supreme evidence of German courage, manhood, and Kultur.

But as we view the thing without passion we must see it without illusion. If the German idea prevails, all that we believe in government, in humanity, in the thing we call civilization, is doomed. If Germany succeeds in this war then it is not again time, as Pitt said after Austerlitz, 'To roll up the map of Europe,' but it is time to burn our ancient parchments and dismiss our hard won faith. All that there is in the German idea was expressed in the *Lusitania* Massacre, it was expressed in the killing of women and children, innocent of all offense, entitled to all protection as helpless, unoffending, as the children of a race not at war, at least entitled to immunity which hitherto was reckoned the right of women and children, neutral or belligerent.

The war that is being fought in Europe is a war for civilization. The battle of Great Britain, of France, of Russia, is our battle. If it is lost, we shall return to the standards and the faiths of other centuries. The truth of this is written in the wreck of the *Lusitania,* it is written in the wreck of Belgium and the desert of Northern France for those who may see. Where the German has gone he has carried physical death, but he has done more, he has carried spiritual death to all that is essential in our own democratic faith, which derives from that of Britain and France.

This war in Europe is going on until the German idea is crushed or conquers. The world cannot now exist half civilized and half German. Only one of two conceptions of life, of humanity, can subsist. One of the conceptions was written in the *Lusitania* Massacre, written clear beyond all mistaking. It is this writing that we should study on this anniversary; it is this fact that we should grasp today, not in anger, not in any spirit that clamors for vengeance, but as the citizens of a nation which has inherited noble ideals and gallant traditions, which has inherited liberty and light from those who died to serve them, and now stands face to face with that which seeks to extinguish both throughout the world.

Vae Victis! and *War Has Its Compensations*

HENRY WATTERSON
Louisville (Ky.) *Courier-Journal*

FROM the time World War I commenced in 1914, Henry Watterson, 74-year-old editor of the *Louisville Courier-Journal,* was the American press's leading exponent of American entry. In that year he had given a war cry to those Americans favoring the Allies: "To Hell with the Hohenzollerns and the Hapsburgs." When the United States entered the war in 1917, what Watterson had been urging for three years became reality. To celebrate the event, Watterson penned two editorials. Both are typical of Watterson's sonorous, flowery, marching style. When the Pulitzer committee met during a time of patriotic fervor to select the award for editorial writing, it gave Watterson's editorials a unanimous vote. The editorials, the judges declared, "were directed toward arousing the American people to their international duty and toward convincing a section of the country by tradition hostile to universal military service of the wisdom and necessity of its establishment." Now classic is the surprised and delighted "Marse Henry's" reply when informed of the award: "The gander-legged boys in the City Editor's room will find out that the old man is a promising journalist." He sent the $500 prize money to a war fund.

VAE VICTIS!
(APRIL 7, 1917)

"Rally round the flag, boys"—Uncle Sam's Battle song;
"Sound the bold anthem! War dogs are howling;
Proud bird of Liberty screams through the air!"

—The Hunters of Kentucky

IT is with solemnity, and a touch of sadness, that we write the familiar words of the old refrain beneath the invocation to the starry banner, the breezy call of hero-breeding bombast quite gone out of them; the glad shout of battle; the clarion note of defiance; because to us, not as to Nick of the Woods, and his homely co-mates of the forest, but rather as to the men of '61, comes this present call to arms.

We may feel with the woman's heart of Rankin of Montana, yet repudiate with manly disdain the sentimental scruples of Kitchin of North Carolina.

There are times when feeling must be sent to the rear; when duty must toe the line; when the aversion brave men have for fighting must yield to the adjuration, "Give me liberty, or give me death!" That time is now upon us.

Unless Patrick Henry was wrong—unless Washington and the men of the Revolution were wrong, that time is upon us. It is a lie to pretend that the world is better than it was; that men are truer, wiser; that war is escapable; that peace may be had for the planning and the asking. The situation which without any act of ours rises before us is as exigent as that which rose before the Colonists in America when a mad English King, claiming to rule without accountability, asserted the right of Kings and sent an army to enforce it. A mad German Emperor, claiming partnership with God, again elevates the standard of right divine and bids the world to worship, or die.

From the beginning the issue was not less ours than of the countries first engaged. Each may have had ends of its own to serve. Nor were these ends precisely alike. At least France—to whom we owe all that we have of sovereignty and freedom—and Belgium, the little David of Nations—fought to resist invasion, wanton, cruel invasion; to avert slavery, savage, pitiless slavery. Yet, whatever the animating purpose—whatever the selfish interests of England and Russia and Italy—the Kaiser scheme of world conquest justified it.

In us it sanctifies it. Why should any American split hairs over the European rights and wrongs involved when he sees before him grim and ghastly the mailed figure of Absolutism with hand uplifted to strike Columbia where these three years she has stood pleading for justice, peace, and mercy? God of the free heart's hope and home forbid!

Each of these three years the German Kaiser was making war upon us. He was making war secretly, through his emissaries in destruction of our industries, secretly through his diplomats plotting not merely foreign but civil war against us, and, as we now know, seeking to foment servile and racial insurrection; then openly upon the high seas levying murder upon our people and visiting all our rights and claims with scorn and insult—with scorn and insult unspeakable—at this moment pretending to flout us with ignominy and contempt. Where would the honest passivist draw the line?

Surely the time has arrived—many of us think it was long since overdue—for calling the braves to the colors. Nations must e'en take stock on occasion and manhood come to a showdown. It is but a truism to say so.

Fifty years the country has enjoyed surpassing prosperity. This has over-commercialized the character and habits of the people. Twenty-five years the gospel of passivism, with "business is business" for its text, has not only been preached—indiscriminately—oracularly without let or hindrance, but has been richly financed and potentially organized. It has established a party. It has made a cult, justifying itself in a fad it has called Humanity—in many ways a most spurious humanity—and has set this above and against patriotic inclination and duty.

Like a bolt out of the blue flashed the war signal from the very heart of Europe. Across the Atlantic its reverberations rolled to find us divided, neutral, and unprepared. For fifteen years a body of German reservists disguised as citizens have been marching and counter-marching. They grew at length bold enough to rally to the support of a pan-German scheme of conquest and a pro-German propaganda of "kultur," basing its effrontery in the German-American vote, which began its agitation by threatening us with civil war if we dared to go to war with Germany. There followed the assassin sea monsters and the airship campaign of murder.

All the while we looked on with either simpering idiocy or dazed apathy. Serbia? It was no affair of ours. Belgium? Why should we worry? Foodstuffs soaring—war stuffs roaring—everybody making money—the mercenary, the poor of heart, the mean of spirit, the bleak and barren of soul, could still plead the Hypocrisy of Uplift and chortle: "I did not raise my boy to be a soldier." Even the *Lusitania* did not awaken us to a sense of danger and arouse us from the stupefaction of ignorant and ignoble self-complacency.

First of all on bended knee we should Pray to God to forgive us. Then erect as men, Christian men, soldierly men, to the flag and the fray wherever they lead us—over the ocean—through France to Flanders—across the Low Countries to Koln, Bonn and Koblenz—tumbling the fortress of Ehrenbreitstein into the Rhine as we pass and damming the mouth of the Moselle with the debris of the ruin we make of it—then on, on to Berlin, the Black Horse Cavalry sweeping the Wilhelmstrasse like lava down the mountain side, the Junker and the saber rattler flying before us, the tunes being "Dixie" and "Yankee Doodle," the cry being "Hail the French Republic—Hail the Republic of Russia—welcome the Commonwealth of the Vaterland—no peace with the Kaiser—no parley with Autocracy, Absolutism and the divine right of Kings—to Hell with the Hapsburg and the Hohenzollern!"

WAR HAS ITS COMPENSATIONS
(APRIL 10, 1917)

THE man who is for peace at any price—who will fight on no provocation—for no cause—is apt to be either what men call "a poor creature," or an impostor set on by ulterior considerations. He may have an unworthy motive, or a selfish interest, or he may be a victim of the coward's fear of battle, or be obsessed by the doctrinaire's theory of universal brotherhood. But, craven or crank, or scheming rogue, he dishonors the noble heritage of manhood which, being common to us all, is only prized and extolled in conspicuous cases of sacrifice or prowess.

Pacifism, as it has shown itself in these times of emergency, has been compounded of each of these ingredients. But it would not have shown itself so strong if it had not been definitely organized, nor definitely organized if it had not been sufficiently financed. The Hague Arbitration movement, backed in this country by the Carnegie Foundation—actually started by the dethroned Czar of Russia—proposed a benefaction to humankind which few if any were disposed to question. It built itself upon a generally accepted truth. The gospel of "peace on earth, goodwill to men," was preached as never before. Professional warriors arrayed themselves in its behalf. Civilized nations flocked to the new religion and raised the benign standard. Many treaties embodying its aims were negotiated. One, and one alone, of the great Powers held out. That was Germany. Why, we now see clearly what we then did not see at all.

How much, if any, of the Carnegie Foundation money has been applied to the recent agitations against war with Germany, we know not. The activities of Mr. Bryan and of Dr. Jordan would lead to the conclusion that it has not been idle, or grudging, since neither of them works for nothing. But it is quite certain that it has been cunningly supplemented and enormously increased by money sent from Berlin to maintain a propaganda to divide our people and paralyze our Government. The prosecution of this now becomes treason and a pacifist who adheres to it is a traitor.

The conspirator who, claiming to be a pacifist, engaged in the nefarious business will be at no loss to save his skin. If he be a German emissary sent over for the purpose he has only to slip away. If he be a Kaiser reservist masquerading as an American citizen he can shift his foot and change his coat. If he be a selfish politician of the Stone–La Follette variety, with an eye on the Hyphenated Vote, he can wink his other eye, hoist the flag and sing "The Star-Spangled Banner" as lustily as the rest.

Those who are most in danger and only in danger are the honest simpletons who stick to it that war is crime; that we have no case against Germany, but, if we have, that it will keep; who go around mouthing socialistic and infidelistic platitudes about a paradisiac dreamland which exists nowhere outside their muddled brains. They cannot see that we have pursued peace to the limit and that peace longer pursued will prove more costly than war. Perverse and egotistical, prompted by the half truths of defective education, uninspired by ideals having any relation to the state of the country, or the spiritual needs of existence, they will not stop their vain chatter until, obstructing enlistments, or menacing public works, they land in jail.

It is grievous that this should be so. Yet it were not occasion for serious comment except that there is a middle class of non-descripts who are more numerous than an earnest and luminous patriotism would have them; men, who were born without enthusiasm and have lived to make money; men, with whom "business is business"; men who are indifferent to what happens so it does not happen to them; in short, men who recall the citation from "The Cricket on the Hearth," put into the mouth of Caleb Plummer:

There was a jolly miller and he lived upon the Dee.
He sang to himself, "I care for nobody and nobody cares for me."

"A most equivocal jollity," as Dickens does not fail to remark.

These people have sprung from the over-commercialism of fifty years of a kind of uncanny prosperity. Their example has affected injuriously the nation's reputation and has trenched perilously upon the character and habits of the people. It needs to be checked. They need a lesson. Nothing short of the dire exigencies which have come upon us would reach a mass so dense and stoic, so paltry and sordid, so unworthy of the blessings which the heroism of the fathers has secured them. That check and lesson they are about to receive. War is not wholly without its compensations.

The woman who is for peace at any price—whose imagination is filled with the horror of war—who, true to her nature, shrinks from bloodshed—is not as the man who skulks from the line and lowers alike the flag of his country and manhood. Ah, no! Peace is the glory of woman. Not upon the soul-stirring field of battle—the [sic] rather in the dread field hospital after the battle—are her trophies to be found.

Well may she stand out against the strife of nations—yet equally with brave men she has her place in the orbit of duty and valor—and, when there is no peace, when war has come, the woman who whines "I did not raise my boy to be a soldier" forfeits her right and claim to be considered only a little lower than the angels, dishonors the genius of Womanhood and removes herself from the company and category of the heroic mothers of the world.

War, horrible as war is—"Hell," as a great warrior said it was—is not without its compensations. No man has more than one time to die. In bringing the realization of death nearer to us war throws a new light upon life. The soldier is a picked man. Whether he be a soldier in arms or a soldier of the cross, his courage, his loyalty, his love and faith challenge the confidence of men and the adoration of women. If he falls he has paid his mortal debt with honor. If he survives, though crippled, he is not disabled. His crutch tells its own story and carries its mute appeal, and there is an eloquence, though silent, resistless, in the empty sleeve.

Christendom stands face to face with the dispersion of some of its cherished ideals. There is much in its Bible that must needs be retranslated and readjusted. Although this will arouse the theologians, they will have to meet it.

Where this present cataclysm will leave us no man can foresee. Our world is, and will still remain, a world of sin, disease and death. This no man can deny. Science is minimizing disease. Death being certain, can creeds or statutes extirpate sin? Can they change the nature of man?

Before all else they must chasten it. For two thousand years theologic controversy has not only kept the world at war, but has driven its inhabitants further apart. It may be that this world war has come to cleanse the earth and to bring all tribes and races to a better understanding of what Christendom is, since there is no reason to doubt that the essential principles of Christianity will continue to dominate the universe.

'Tis a long way, we are told, to the Tipperary of Hibernia, but yet a longer [way] to the Millennial Tipperary of Scriptural mythology. The Christ-child must be born again in the heart of man. At this moment it is not the star of Bethlehem that shines. It is the luminary of the war god. The drums beat as for the men of old. "To your tents, O Israel," comes the word out of the deeps of the far away, and from highway and byway, as if in answer, the refrain "Tramp, tramp, tramp, the boys are marching."

Yet the Associated Press dispatches carry the following:

Washington, April 7.—Continuation of the pacifist fight on President Wilson's war programme was forecast to-day when the fifty Representatives who voted against the war resolution received the following identic telegram from Lelia Fay Secor, secretary of the Emergency Peace Federation:

"On behalf of the Emergency Peace Federation I thank you for your patriotic stand in opposition to war. May I request that you communicate at once with Representative Kitchin, to whom I have written a letter suggesting co-operation between ourselves and the pacifists in congress."

Mr. Kitchin is at his home in North Carolina and details of the scheme outlined in the letter to him could not be learned. He announced before leaving Washington that his opposition to the war programme would end with his vote against the resolution.

"Scissors!" shrieks Lelia Fay.

"Scissors!" cries good Mrs. Garrison Villard.

And away off yonder from the limb of a tree the Dickey Bird, impersonated by Claude Kitchin, responds, "Not on your life, ladies!"

Law and the Jungle

(SEPTEMBER 30, 1919)

1920

HARVEY E. NEWBRANCH
Omaha (Neb.) *Evening World-Herald*

IN September 1919 a Negro man was arrested for the rape of a white woman in Omaha, Nebraska. A mob gathered, broke the man from jail and lynched him. This episode and the rioting that followed are chronicled in this editorial by Harvey Newbranch, editor of the *Evening World-Herald.* It was the first of numerous Pulitzer Prize editorials on the theme of law-and-order during racial crises. None of the later ones has surpassed the quality of Newbranch's work. While passion burns in the words, the editorial still exhibits a well-defined logic. The polarity between lawlessness and obedience to the law is clearly stated. A number of themes discussed are worth considering because they are common in later Pulitzer editorials, themes dealing, for example, with the necessity of obedience to law, the injustice of racial prejudice, the shame of rioters as cowards and animals, the blaming of authorities for their failure to uphold the law, and the appeal to civic pride in the good reputation of a town.

THERE is the rule of the jungle in this world, and there is the rule of law.

Under jungle rule no man's life is safe, no man's wife, no man's mother, sister, children, home, liberty, rights, property. Under the rule of law protection is provided for all these, and provided in proportion as law is efficiently and honestly administered and its power and authority respected and obeyed.

Omaha Sunday was disgraced and humiliated by a monstrous object lesson of what jungle rule means. The lack of efficient government in Omaha, the lack of governmental foresight and sagacity and energy, made the exhibition possible. It was provided by a few hundred hoodlums, most of them mere boys, organized as the wolf-pack is organized, inflamed by the spirit of anarchy and license, of plunder and destruction. Ten thousand or more good citizens, without leadership, without organization, without public authority that had made an effort to organize them for the anticipated emergency, were obliged to stand as onlookers, shamed in their hearts, and witness the hideous orgy of lawlessness. Some of them, to their blighting shame be it said, respectable men with women and children in their homes, let themselves be swept away by the mob spirit. They encouraged if they did not aid the wolf-pack that was conspiring to put down the rule of law in Omaha—that rule which is the sole protection for every man's home and family.

It is over now, thank God!

Omaha henceforth will be as safe for its citizens, and as safe for the visitors within its gates, as any city in the land. Its respectable and law-abiding people, comprising 99 per cent of the population, will see to that. They have already taken the steps to see to it. The first step was taken when the rioting was at its height—taken belatedly, it is true, because they had placed reliance on the public authorities to safeguard the order and good name of Omaha. The blistering disgrace of the riot has aroused them. There will be no more faltering, no more fickleness, no more procrastination, no longer the lack of a firm hand. The military aid that has been called in is only temporary. It serves to insure public order and public safety for the day, for the week. But the strengthening of the police force of the city, its efficient organization under wise and competent leadership, is a policy that public sentiment has inaugurated and that it will sternly enforce. As to that there will be neither equivocation nor delay. Nor will there be any hesitancy or laxness in the organization, and rigid use if need be, of civic guards to keep the streets and homes and public places of Omaha secure.

The citizenship of Omaha will be anxious that the outside world should know what it was that happened and why it happened. Let there be no mistaking the plain facts. The trouble is over now. It was a flare-up that died as quickly as it was born. Omaha is today the same safe and orderly city it has always been. It will be safer, indeed, hereafter, and more orderly, because of the lesson it has so dearly learned. And the flare-up was the work—let this fact be emphasized—of a few hundred rioters, some of them incited by an outrageous deed, others of them skulkers in the anarchistic underbrush who urged them on for their own foul purposes of destroying property and paralyzing the arm of the law. If the miserable negro, Brown, had been removed from Omaha in time, as he should have been; if, failing to remove him, the public authorities had taken vigorous measures to prevent the congregation and inflaming of the mob, the riot would never have occurred. An organized and intelligently directed effort in advance would have preserved the good name of Omaha untarnished. It would have prevented the lynching. It would have saved our splendid new court house from being offered up in flames, its defense with the mob-victim in it, a costly sacrifice on the altar of law and order. There would have been no thought, even, of the amazing attempt to lynch the mayor of Omaha, bravely and honorably discharging his duty as chief magistrate in resisting the wolf-pack.

It would be impossible to speak too strongly in condemnation of the rioters or in the uncompromising demand for their stern and swift punishment, whoever they be, wherever they can be found. They not only foully murdered a negro they believed to be guilty. They brutally maltreated and attempted to murder other negroes whom they knew to be innocent. They tried to lynch the mayor. They wantonly pillaged stores and destroyed property. They burned the court house. In the sheer spirit of anarchy they pulled valuable records from their steel filing cases, saturated them in gasoline, and burned them. They burned police conveyances and cut the fire hose, inviting the destruction by fire of the entire city. Their actions were wholly vile, wholly evil, and malignantly dangerous. There is not a one of them who can be apprehended, and whose guilt can be proved, but should be sent for a long term to the state prison. And toward that end every effort of every good citizen, as well as every effort of the public authorities, from the humblest policeman to the presiding judge on the bench, must be directed. There can be no sentimentalizing, no fearful hesitancy, no condoning the offense of these red-handed criminals. The pitiful bluff they have put up against the majesty of the law, against the inviolability of American institutions, must be called and called fearlessly.

To the law-abiding negroes of Omaha, who, like the law-abiding whites, are the vast majority of their race, it is timely to speak a word of sympathy and support. Any effort on the part of any of them to take the law into their own hands would be as culpable and as certainly disastrous as was the effort of the mob. In the running down and maltreating of unoffending men of their color, merely because they were of that color, they have been done odious wrong. They naturally and properly resent having been confined to their homes, in trembling fear of their lives, while red riot ran the streets of the city. But their duty as good citizens is precisely the same as that of the rest of us, all of us, who have been outraged and shamed as citizens. It is to look to the law for their protection, for their vindication, and to give the law every possible support as it moves in its course. The law is their only shield, as it is the only shield of every white man, no matter how lowly or how great. And it is the duty of all, whites and blacks alike, to uphold especially the might of the law—to insist, if need be, on its full exercise—in protecting every colored citizen of Omaha in his lawful and constitutional rights.

For the first time in many years—and for the last time, let us hope, for many years to come—Omaha has had an experience with lawlessness. We have seen what it is. We have seen how it works. We have felt, however briefly, the fetid breath of anarchy on our cheeks. We have experienced the cold chill of fear which it arouses. We have seen, as in a nightmare, its awful possibilities. We have learned how frail is the barrier which divides civilization from the primal jungle—and we have been given to see clearly what that barrier is.

It is the Law! It is the Might of the Law, wisely and fearlessly administered! It is respect for and obedience to the Law on the part of the members of society!

When these fail us all things fail. When these are lost all will be lost. Should the day ever come when the rule that was in Omaha Sunday night become the dominant rule, the grasses of the jungle would overspread our civilization, its wild denizens, human and brute, would make their foul feast on the ruins, and the God who rules over us would turn His face in sorrow from a world given over to bestiality.

May the lesson of Sunday night sink deep! May we take home to our hearts, there to be cherished and never for a moment forgotten, the words of the revered Lincoln:

Let reverence of the law be breathed by every mother to the lisping babe that prattles on her lap; let it be taught in schools, seminaries and colleges; let it be written in primers, spelling books and almanacs; let it be preached from pulpits and proclaimed in legislative halls and enforced in courts of justice; let it become the political religion of the nation.

The Unknown Soldier

(NOVEMBER 11, 1921)

FRANK M. O'BRIEN
New York Herald

THE subject of the fourth winner of the Pulitzer Prize for
Editorial Writing was the burial of America's "Unknown
Soldier" November 11, 1921, in Arlington Cemetery. It was
an opportune subject for journalism awards; Kirke Simpson's
1922 Pulitzer for reporting was given also for stories about
the burial. Frank O'Brien's editorial is more emotional and
perhaps more "artistic" than those of today, but despite the
emotionalism of the subject the editorial really has a very
simple, formal structure. Its lead sentence states the three
meanings of the burial, and the body simply explains each in
order. The first two paragraphs are devoted to the "symbol"
(of "Duty and Honor"), the next two to the "mystery" (who
was the "Unknown"?), and the final two long paragraphs and
summary sentence to the "tribute" (the exaltation of the
eternal life of the dead). The editorial's appeal comes from
its nobleness of ideas and the universality of O'Brien's
descriptions. The religious motif, almost unheard of in recent
editorials, is common among early winners of the Pulitzer
Prize.

THAT which takes place today at the National Cemetery in Arlington is a
symbol, a mystery and a tribute. It is an entombment only in the physical
sense. It is rather the enthronement of Duty and Honor. This man who
died for his country is the symbol of these qualities; a far more perfect
symbol than any man could be whose name and deeds we knew. He
represents more, really, than the unidentified dead, for we cannot
separate them spiritually from the war heroes whose names are written
on their gravestones. He—this spirit whom we honor—stands for the
unselfishness of all.

This, of all monuments to the dead, is lasting and immutable. So
long as men revere the finer things of life the tomb of the nameless hero
will remain a shrine. Nor, with the shifts of time and mind, can there be a
changing of values. No historian shall rise to modify the virtues or the
faults of the Soldier. He has an immunity for which kings might pray. The

years may bring erosion to the granite but not to the memory of the Unknown.

It is a common weakness of humanity to ask the questions that can never be answered in this life. Probably none to whom the drama of the Unknown Soldier has appealed has not wondered who, in the sunshine of earth, was the protagonist of today's ceremony. A logger from the Penobscot? An orchardist from the Pacific coast? A well driller from Texas? A machinist from Connecticut? A lad who left his hoe to rust among the Missouri corn? A longshoreman from Hell's Kitchen? Perhaps some youth from the tobacco fields, resting again in his own Virginia. All that the army tells of him is that he died in battle. All that the heart tells is that some woman loved him. More than that no man shall learn. In this mystery, as in the riddle of the universe, the wise wonder; but they would [sic] not know.

What were his dreams, his ambitions? Likely he shared those common to the millions: a life of peace and honest struggle, with such small success as comes to most who try; and at the end the place on the hillside among his fathers. Today to do honor at his last resting place come the greatest soldiers of the age, famous statesmen from other continents, the President, the high judges and the legislators of his own country, and many men who, like himself, fought for the flag. At his bier will gather the most remarkable group that America has seen. And the tomb which Fate reserved for him is, instead of the narrow cell on the village hillside, one as lasting as that of Rameses and as inspiring as Napoleon's.

It is a great religious ceremony, this burial today. The exaltation of the nameless bones would not be possible except for Belief. Where were Duty and Honor, the wellsprings of Victory, if mankind feared that death drew a black curtain behind which lay nothing but the dark? So all in whom the spark of hope has not died can well believe that we, to whom the Soldier is a mystery, are not a mystery to him. They can believe that the watchers at Arlington today are not merely a few thousands of the living but the countless battalions of the departed. "Though he were dead, yet shall he live"—there is the promise to which men hold when everything of this earth has slipped away.

All the impressive ritual of today would be a mockery if we did not believe that, out in an infinity which astronomers cannot chart or mathematicians bound, the Unknown Soldier and all the glorious dead whom we honor in his dust are looking down upon this little spinning ball, conscious of our reverence. And when noon strikes, signal for the moment of silent prayer, few of those who stand with bared head will lack conviction that the rites at Arlington are viewed by other than mortal eyes. Only in that spirit may we honor the Unknown Soldier and those who, like him, died for this Republic.

Unknown, but not unknowing!

To an Anxious Friend

(JULY 27, 1922)

WILLIAM ALLEN WHITE

Emporia (Kan.) *Gazette*

WHEN railroad workers struck in 1922, the governor of Kansas attempted to use the full force of law and his office to suppress the strike. Placards that strikers asked merchants to display in support of the strike offended the governor, Henry Allen, and he ordered them down. William Allen White, a personal friend of the governor, told him the order was a violation of the First Amendment and that White was intending to display a placard himself. "If you do that," Governor Allen threatened, "I'll have to arrest you." White answered, "Come on and arrest me, and we'll test this matter in the courts." He posted in his newspaper office window a placard similar to the type the governor had banned, and the confrontation between the two men became national news. Fred J. Atwood, a close friend of White, wrote the editor a warm and sincere letter to protest. White answered him, and then realized his answer to Atwood would be an answer to all people opposing White's stand. The answer echoes familiar reasoning on the importance of freedom of expression during times of stress. White's writing style, however, comes across clearly and lends impact to the thought. "I worked over the phraseology of that editorial," White explained. "I cut out every adjective and used a verb instead, which greatly strengthens one's style. I shortened it, avoiding repetition, and finally ran it out." The editorial was picked up nationwide because, White surmised, "the moderation and strength of this boiled-down, concentrated, passionate reply to my opponents gave it wings." The strike soon ended, and the governor's suit against White was dropped.

YOU tell me that law is above freedom of utterance. And I reply that you can have no wise laws nor free enforcement of wise laws unless there is free expression of the wisdom of the people—and alas, their folly with it. But if there is freedom, folly will die of its own poison, and the wisdom will survive. That is the history of the race. It is the proof of man's kinship with God. You say that freedom of utterance is not for time of stress, and I reply with the sad truth that only in time of stress is freedom of utterance in danger. No one questions it in calm days, because it is not needed. And the reverse is true also; only when free utterance is suppressed is it needed, and when it is needed, it is most vital to justice.

Peace is good. But if you are interested in peace through force and without free discussion—that is to say, free utterance decently and in order—your interest in justice is slight. And peace without justice is tyranny, no matter how you may sugar coat it with expediency. This state today is in more danger from suppression than from violence, because in the end, suppression leads to violence. Violence, indeed, is the child of Suppression. Whoever pleads for justice helps to keep the peace; and whoever tramples upon the plea for justice, temperately made in the name of peace, only outrages peace and kills something fine in the heart of man which God put there when we got our manhood. When that is killed, brute meets brute on each side of the line.

So, dear friend, put fear out of your heart. This nation will survive, this state will prosper, the orderly business of life will go forward if only men can speak in whatever way given them to utter what their hearts hold—by voice, by posted card, by letter or by press. Reason never has failed men. Only force and repression have made the wrecks in the world.

Who Made Coolidge?
(SEPTEMBER 14, 1923)

FRANK BUXTON
Boston Herald

THE announcement of the 1924 winner of the Pulitzer Prize
was met with criticism. Frank Buxton's editorial, written shortly after Calvin Coolidge had become president on the death of
Warren G. Harding, repeatedly asks the question, "Who made
Coolidge?" and each time gives a short answer. The criticisms
that can be made of it are that its thought is superficial and its
form simple. *Editor and Publisher* said of it: "The editorial prize
winner seems to us a labored effort, freakish, without deep
penetration and lacking qualities of spontaneity and purpose
that one would expect in an editorial selected for distinguished
merit from the year's production. The author might have carried his musical inquiry back to the biological source of human
existence." But on the positive side, it can be argued that the
editorial is not typical of most editorial style or structure. Its
mood is a pleasing combination of humor and adulation. Rather
than being superficial, one could argue, its reasoning does attempt to get at fundamental factors in Coolidge's rise to the
presidency. This rise, the editorial implies, was the result of a
combination of Coolidge's acquaintances, his character, and
happenstance. It recognizes the essentials of Coolidge's gaining
national prominence: his honesty and frugality, his handling of
the Boston police strike of 1919, the political astuteness of
Frank Stearns and Senator W. Murray Crane, and the long line
of accidents favoring his fortunes.

"WHO made Calvin Coolidge?"

Margaret Foley, of course. When Levis Grenwood was President of
the Massachusetts Senate he opposed woman suffrage. She opposed his
re-election in his district and prevailed. Senator Coolidge became President Coolidge on Beacon Hill and the signals were set clear for the road to
the Governorship.

"Who made Calvin Coolidge?"

Edwin U. Curtis, of course. When he was a sick man in that old
brick building at the dead-end of Pemberton Square, the heedless policemen went on strike to the refrain, "Hail, Hail, the Gang's All Here."

The sick man showed the strength of the stalwart, until finally Governor Coolidge sent a telegram to Samuel Gompers that tapped its way into national prominence, and is today a sort of Magna Charta of the people's rights.

"Who made Calvin Coolidge?"

James Lucey, the Northampton cobbler, of course. No explanation or argument is necessary here, but merely a reminder. The *Herald* published a facsimile a few days ago of President Coolidge's letter to him, which said: "If it were not for you, I should not be here."

"Who made Calvin Coolidge?"

Frank W. Stearns, of course. With as close an approximation to second sight as we may expect in these days, and with an ability to see around the corner years before Einstein told us how rays of light are bent, this substantial, self-made, self-respecting Boston merchant, with his quiet sense of obligation to the community, discerned qualities which hardly anyone else glimpsed. To go to the Republican Convention he left a Governor only to come back to pay his respects to a potential Vice-President.

"Who made Calvin Coolidge?"

Senator Crane, of course. He made Coolidge by showing him, in precept and practice, the way of wisdom and by vouching for him in high places where his chance say-so was as good as his oath and bond. To the younger man he gave that mixture of personal attachment and respect of which he was none too prodigal, but always of mighty advantage to the few who won it.

"Who made Calvin Coolidge?"

The Republican Party of Massachusetts, of course, a canny organization, with some Bourbonism, some democracy, some vision, some solid traditions and no end of genuine appreciation of the merits of a trustworthy man. It always lined up behind him solidly even when he displayed that reticence which to the unknowing was some evidence of ingratitude, and to the knowing was merely Coolidgeism.

"Who made Calvin Coolidge?"

The people of Massachusetts, of course. They took him at more than his own modest valuation, whether he wanted to be a town officer or a Governor. They had that which thousands call a blind faith in him. More thousands called it a passionate intuition.

"Who made Calvin Coolidge?"

His mother, of course, who endowed him with her own attributes; a father that taught him prudential ways with all the quiet vigor of the old Greeks, who preached moderation in everything; his school and his college; his classmate, Dwight Morrow; and his guest of a day or two ago at the White House, William F. Whiting.

"Who made Calvin Coolidge?"

Calvin Coolidge, of course. From the reflective shoemaker and the furious Miss Foley to the complacent Frank W. Stearns and the watchful and discerning Senator from Dalton came some of the makings, but the man himself had the essentials of greatness. Give another man those same foes and friends and he might still be as far from the White House as most sons of Vermont.

The Plight of the South

(NOVEMBER 5, 1924)

ROBERT LATHAN

Charleston (S.C.) *News & Courier*

IN the 1920s the South was a neglected political region, offering no programs of national importance and receiving no acknowledgment in return. Its peculiar racial situation obscured its view and interest in other issues, and it had no strong political leaders capable of or interested in focusing its mind and strength on other areas. As a result, other sections ignored it politically and it suffered neglect in national programs. Much of the problem was created by the Southern mentality of peculiarity and isolation. Most newspapers did little to ameliorate the problem, looking at it from the same perspective as their readers and seeing little need for change. It was to stimulate awareness of this problem that Robert Lathan, editor of the *Charleston* (S.C.) *News & Courier,* wrote "The Plight of the South." Lathan emphasizes particularly the void in national political programs and leadership coming out of the South. His editorial does not attempt to provide solutions to the problem— it simply presents and analyzes the situation, but with an obvious desire that answers be found.

THIS article is being written on election day but before the result of the voting can possibly be known. No matter. The suggestions it contains will still be pertinent whatever the story told by the first page this morning. It makes very little difference what any of us think about the outcome of yesterday's balloting. It makes a considerable difference whether or not the people of the South realize the precarious situation which this section has come to occupy politically.

As yet we doubt if very many of them do realize this; and yet it is, we think, the outstanding political development of the time so far as we are concerned. Look at the facts. They are not pleasant to contemplate but they cannot be ignored longer. We are in a sad fix politically in this part of the country and if we are to find a remedy for our troubles we must first of all determine what they are. That will take considerable discussion and all we can hope to do now is to help start the ball of this discussion rolling. If that can be accomplished we may achieve the new program and the new leadership which we so much need.

For at the root of the South's present plight lies the fact that it has today virtually no national program and virtually no national leadership. Is it strange that it should be treated by the rest of the country as such a negligible factor? What is it contributing today in the way of political thought? What political leaders has it who possess weight or authority beyond their own States? What constructive policies are its people ready to fight for with the brains and zeal that made them a power in the old days?

The Plight of the South in these respects would be perilous at any time. In a period when political currents are deeper and swifter than ever before, with more violent whirlpools, more dangerous rocks and shoals, ours is truly a perilous position. Changes which used to be decades in the making now sweep over us almost before we know they are in contemplation. It is true everywhere. In all the countries of Europe the pendulum is swinging, now far to the left, now far to the right. Center parties have lost their power. They are in a very bad way. And the South has belonged to the school politically which sought as a rule the middle of the road, eschewing ultra-conservatism on the one hand and radicalism on the other. With Labor organized and militant, with radicalism organized and in deadly earnest, with conservatism organized and drawing the lines sharply, what is the South to do, what course shall she take, where do her interests lie, what is due to happen to her?

These are questions which already begin to press for answers. Who is to speak for the South? How many of her citizens are prepared to help formulate her replies?

The House of a Hundred Sorrows

(DECEMBER 14, 1925)

EDWARD M. KINGSBURY
New York Times

THE *New York Times,* like many other newspapers, has been in the habit of compiling a list of neediest people in their city and sponsoring drives to help them during the Christmas season. The problem for the editorial writer sometimes is how to write a yearly piece supporting such a campaign. For his editorial urging help with the *Times*'s "One Hundred Neediest," Edward M. Kingsbury won a Pulitzer Prize. While the editorial may be criticized for its simplicity and artificiality, it also shows true sympathy and concern for the needy. Edward P. Mitchell, editor of the *New York Sun,* of which Kingsbury had been a staff member, said Kingsbury was unique for his "exquisite humor, fine wit, broad literary appreciation and originality of idea and phrase." The executive secretary of the Pulitzer Advisory Board said that though the Pulitzer Prize was awarded to Kingsbury on the basis of his "brilliant" previous work, the award was made primarily because of this one "beautiful" editorial.

THE walls are grimy and discolored. The uneven floors creak and yield under foot. Staircases and landings are rickety and black. The door of every room is open. Walk along these corridors. Walk into this room. Here is a sickly boy of 5, deserted by his mother, underfed, solitary in the awful solitude of starved neglected childhood. "Seldom talks." Strange, isn't it? Some, many children, never "prattle," like your darlings. They are already old. They are full, perhaps, of long, hopeless thoughts. There are plenty of other "kids" in this tenement. Here is one, only 3. Never saw his father. His mother spurned and abused him. He is weak and "backward." How wicked of him when he has been so encouraged and coddled! Do children play? Not his kind. They live to suffer.

In Room 24 is Rose, a housemother of 10. Father is in the hospital. Mother is crippled with rheumatism. Rose does all the work. You would love Rose if she came out of Dickens. Well, there she is, mothering her mother in Room 24. In Room 20 age has been toiling for youth. Grandmother has been taking care of three granddaughters who lost their mother. A brave old woman; but what with rheumatism and heart weakness, threescore-and-ten can't go out to work any more. What's going to happen to her and her charges? Thinking of that, she is ill on top of her physical illness. A very interesting house, isn't it, Sir? Decidedly "a rum sort of place," Madam? Come into Room 23. Simon, the dollmaker— but handmade dolls are "out"—lives, if you call it living, here. Eighty years old, his wife of about the same age. Their eyesight is mostly gone. Otherwise they would still be sewing on buttons and earning a scanty livelihood for themselves and two little girls, their grandchildren. The girls object to going to an orphan home. Some children are like that.

You must see those twin sisters of 65 in Room 47. True, they are doing better than usual on account of the coming holidays; making as much as $10 a month, whereas their average is but $6. Still, rents are a bit high; and the twins have been so long together that they would like to stay so. In Room—but you need no guide. Once in The House of a Hundred Sorrows you will visit every sad chamber in it. If your heart be made of penetrable stuff, you will do the most you can to bring hope and comfort to its inmates, to bring them Christmas and the Christ.

For I was ahungred, and ye gave me meat: I was thirsty, and ye gave me drink: I was a stranger, and ye took me in.

Naked, and ye clothed me: I was sick, and ye visited me: I was in prison, and ye came unto me.

We Submit

(OCTOBER 26, 1926)

F. LAURISTON BULLARD
Boston Herald

IN 1921 the anarchists Nicola Sacco and Bartolomeo Vanzetti, accused of robbing and murdering a shoe factory paymaster, were convicted on what many people considered slender evidence. As execution was delayed six years by one appeal after another, Sacco and Vanzetti became the focus of worldwide attention and of debate over the fundamental nature of the American political system. Radicals and liberals argued that the two were found guilty not for an alleged crime but for their opinions. They cited as one piece of evidence the fact that trial judge Webster Thayer had expressed prejudice against the defendants. But an overwhelming majority of the public favored executing the two. Not only were they anarchists; but Italian immigrants, pacifists, and draft-dodgers, too. It was not popular—especially in Massachusetts, where the murder occurred—to defend them. Despite such public opinion, the *Boston Herald* reversed its original attitude and began calling for a new trial. In a judicious editorial F. Lauriston Bullard argued the paper's point of view. A new trial was not granted, as the editorial urged; but a three-member commission was appointed by the Massachusetts governor, as Bullard suggested, to advise him. The commission, however, refused to propose executive clemency. Sacco and Vanzetti were executed August 22, 1927. Their deaths did not end the controversy; they added fire. The execution, as Bullard had implied in the editorial's final paragraph, gave radicals the argument they needed to persuade believers in justice to extreme positions and forced liberals to question the soundness of American institutions.

IN our opinion Nicola Sacco and Bartolomeo Vanzetti ought not to be executed on the warrant of the verdict returned by a jury on July 14, 1921. We do not know whether these men are guilty or not. We have no sympathy with the half-baked views which they profess. But as months have merged into years and the great debate over this case has continued, our doubts have solidified slowly into convictions, and reluctantly we have found ourselves compelled to reverse our original judgment. We hope the

Supreme Judicial Court will grant a new trial on the basis of the new evidence not yet examined in open court. We hope the Governor will grant another reprieve to Celestino Madeiros so that his confession may be canvassed in open court. We hope, in case our supreme bench finds itself unable legally to authorize a new trial, that our Governor will call to his aid a commission of disinterested men of the highest intelligence and character to make an independent investigation in his behalf, and that the Governor himself at first-hand will participate in that examination if, as a last resort, it shall be undertaken.

We have read the full decision in which Judge Webster Thayer, who presided at the original trial, renders his decision against the application for a new trial, and we submit that it carries the tone of the advocate rather than the arbitrator. At the outset he refers to "the verdict of a jury approved by the Supreme Court of this Commonwealth," and later he repeats that sentence. We respectfully submit that the Supreme Court never approved that verdict. What the court did it stated in its own words thus: "We have examined carefully all the exceptions in so far as argued, and finding no error the verdicts are to stand." The Supreme Court did not vindicate the verdict. The court certified that, whether the verdict was right or wrong, the trial judge performed his duty under the law in a legal manner. The Supreme Court overruled a bill of exceptions, but expressed no judgment whatever as to the validity of the verdict or the guilt of the defendants. Judge Thayer knows this, yet allows himself to refer to the verdict as "approved by the Supreme Court."

We submit, also, that Judge Thayer's language contains many innuendos which surely are unfortunate in such a document. The petition for a new trial is based in part on the affidavits of two men, Letherman and Weyand, connected respectively with the United States Government for thirty-six years and eight years, and both now holding responsible positions out of the Federal service. Judge Thayer says that one of these men "seems for some reason to be willing to go the limit in his affidavits against the government of the United States," and he refers to "prejudiced affidavits, which appear to be quite easily obtained nowadays." The charges are rung on certain phrases also, as "fraudulent conspiracy between these two great governments," meaning the Governments of the United States and Massachusetts. The judge asserts a conspiracy charge which was not made by counsel for the defense; he asks "who pumped this curiosity into Madeiros"; he compliments the prosecution and refers slightingly to counsel for the defense.

We submit that evidence, if any, in the files of the Department of Justice having any bearing on this case ought to be examined in open court, or examined in private by the United States Attorney General and reported upon by him before this case shall finally be decided. We have no idea what the files may contain. Mr. Weyand said in his affidavit: "The conviction was the result of cooperation between the Boston agents of the Department of Justice and the District Attorney." We do not know that this is true, but we know there was cooperation; the department and the attorney joined in placing a spy in the cell next to Sacco's, and the prosecution admitted the fact in court.

Now as to Madeiros: A criminal with a bad record, true, and under sentence of death. But the Government relied in part on one of his confessions to convict him of a murder. His evidence was accepted against himself when his own life was at stake. His evidence now is offered in behalf of two other men whose lives also are at stake. We submit that Madeiros should be placed on the stand in open court, facing a jury and a judge, and subjected to examination and cross-examination. He may be lying, but the criterion here is not what a judge may think about it, but what a jury might think about it. The question is, Would the new evidence be a real factor with a jury in reaching a decision?

We submit that doubt is cast on the verdict of the jury by the important affidavit made after the trial by Captain C. H. Proctor of the State Police. On the stand, testifying as an expert, his evidence was understood by the jury and the judge to be that the fatal bullet issued from Sacco's pistol. Careful examination of the record discloses curious facts. Captain Proctor did not here reply to direct questions. His affidavit states what the record implies, that a device was fixed up in advance for dodging [a] direct answer to a direct question. His replies were understood to mean that he believed the bullet came from that weapon. He allowed that impression to go abroad. But his affidavit contradicts that testimony. Now, when the Supreme Court dealt with that point it expressed no opinion as to whether or not an "ambiguous answer" had been arranged to "obtain a conviction." The court ruled only that the trial judge had decided that no such pre-arrangement had been made, and that the Supreme Court could not "as a matter of law" set aside the ruling of the trial judge.

For these and other reasons we hope that the resources of our laws will prove adequate to obtain a new trial. Let it be remembered that the new trial is asked for on the basis of evidence never before the Supreme Court previously. The court has ruled on exceptions to the old trial, never on all evidence for a new one. If on a new trial the defendants shall again be found guilty we shall be infinitely better off than if we proceed to execution on the basis of the trial already held; the shadow of doubt which abides in the minds of large numbers of patient investigators of this whole case will have been removed. And if on second trial Sacco and Vanzetti should be declared guiltless everybody would rejoice that no monstrous injustice shall have been done. We submit these views with no reference whatever to the personality of the defendants, and without allusion now to that atmosphere of radicalism of which we heard so much in 1921.

We Predict a Freeze

(AUGUST 14, 1927)

(for editorials against gangsterism and brutality)

GROVER CLEVELAND HALL
Montgomery (Ala.) *Advertiser*

THE revival of the Ku Klux Klan became a major problem in the 1920s. In few other places was it as bad as in Alabama, where the Klan gained gruesome control of government at all levels. By 1927, a year in which both of the state's U.S. senators were Klan members, the organization had become daringly bold. The ministry and the press, whose ranks contained a number of KKK sympathizers, remained silent at the Klan's outrages. But the Klan had at least one opponent among Alabama's journalists, Grover C. Hall, editor of the *Montgomery Advertiser*. Born in Alabama in 1888, Hall joined the *Advertiser* in 1910 and was trained in its "tradition of tolerance." He was named editor in 1926. In July of the following year, his anger and indignation ignited by the flogging of a young Negro at a rural church, Hall opened fire on the Klan. He followed with a four-month campaign to bring the responsible Klansmen to justice, to expose the Klan as brutish and cowardly, and to get legislation enacted that would limit its activities, including a law to prohibit the wearing of masks in public. State action did result. As a consequence of Hall's campaign, victims of floggings, too frightened before, talked to law officers and journalists, numerous Klansmen were convicted, and the number of floggings in Alabama declined dramatically. For his campaign, Hall was awarded the 1928 Pulitzer, the first year in which the award was given for no specific editorial but for a series. "We Predict a Freeze" was reprinted by *Editor and Publisher* in 1928, in its story of the Pulitzer Prize awards, as typical of Hall's work. Unlike most other Pulitzer editorials, it is a fine example that an editorial can make a point forcefully with a minimum of words.

THE fiery cross is not a permanent source of heat. It will burn out, leaving only charred remains fit only for use in 4½ gallon kegs. Those politicians

31

who thought it was to be as long-lived as the sun and accordingly resolved to keep themselves warm by it alone, will presently find themselves shivering in the cold. Then if they ask the faithful keepers of the constitutional home-fires for a blanket, they will be given a bedsheet and told to be on their way.

An Unspeakable Act of Savagery

(JUNE 22, 1928)

LOUIS ISAAC JAFFE
Norfolk Virginian-Pilot

IN the 1920s, when the revival of the Ku Klux Klan gave it a bigger heyday than it had enjoyed during Reconstruction, lynchings were considered local offenses. State prosecution had few supporters. A leader of the movement for state anti-lynching laws was Louis Isaac Jaffe, editor of the *Virginian-Pilot*. In the midtwenties he outlined plans for a law in Virginia and finally convinced Governor Harry Flood Byrd to propose a law to the legislature. When the bill was adopted in 1928, Byrd said Jaffe's editorials "had more to do than any other single outside urging in convincing me that I should make one of my major recommendations the passage of a drastic anti-lynching law providing that lynching be a specific state offense." But Jaffe did not rest after enactment of the Virginia law. He urged a national law. Following a lynching in Houston, Texas, on the eve of the 1928 Democratic National Convention, he wrote "An Unspeakable Act of Savagery." Though Congress would delay in enacting antilynching legislation, Jaffe's editorial sparked national interest in such law.

As the Democratic hosts prepare to rededicate themselves anew to fairness and justice, the bustling Southern city in which they are to meet is disgraced by an unspeakable act of savagery. There is no other way to describe the performance of the eight armed white men who yanked Robert Powell, 24-year-old Negro, from a hospital cot on which he lay with a bullet in his stomach, and hanged him from a bridge just outside the city. Powell was under the charge of killing a detective in a shooting match from which he himself emerged with an apparently mortal wound. In the event of his recovery, he was headed for the courts. But to this Texas mob neither Death nor Justice was an acceptable arbiter. Nothing would satisfy them but a loathsome act of murder carried out against a human being while he lay in agony with a bullet in his entrails.

Houston, which is said not to have had a lynching in fifty years, is understandably stirred by this foul thing laid on its doorstep just when it was most anxious to show itself to the world at its cleanest. The City

33

Council made an immediate appropriation of $10,000 for an investigation to be carried out by a committee representative of both races. A grand jury has been ordered to drop all other business to conduct an immediate inquiry. The Governor has offered a reward for the capture of each participant in the lynching and sent a special detail of Texas Rangers to assist the Houston police in the hunt. Apparently the spotlight that beats on Houston at this particular time has had something to do with the energy with which the authorities have acted. Ordinarily, Texas proceeds in these matters with considerably less dispatch and excitement. But this is no time to inquire too closely into motives. One of the proudest cities of Texas has been polluted by one of the foulest forms of mob murder, and it is a matter for general satisfaction that the authorities are moving so energetically to repair the damage to Texas' good name. If the perseverance of the authorities is in keeping with their initial burst of energy, one or more of the group that bravely did to death a crippled man lying on a hospital cot may see the inside of the Texas penitentiary.

The year that saw four months pass without a single lynching has now accumulated five of them. Five lynchings in six months represent a proportional reduction in savagery from last year's record of sixteen lynchings in twelve months, but the year is only half gone and no one may be too confident. We have come a long way from the dark days of 1892 when America celebrated the 400th anniversary of its discovery with 255 lynchings, but we have not yet arrived at that social abhorrence of this crime that must precede its practical extinction. When eight presumably decent and rational beings can gain the consent of their conscience to rob a hospital bed for the purpose of executing summary vengeance, and when, as was the case a few days ago in Louisiana, two Negroes are torn from their guards and lynched because they were brothers of another Negro who was accused of murder, it must be recognized that the rise and fall of the lynching curve is governed by racial passions that remain still to be brought under civilized control.

The Gentleman from Nebraska

(NOVEMBER 7, 1930)

1931

CHARLES S. RYCKMAN
Fremont (Neb.) *Tribune*

SATIRE is rare among the Pulitzer Prize editorials. But while few satirical editorials gleam from the sea of analytical, reasoned prizewinners, they have also been the most controversial. The most biting Pulitzer editorial may have been Charles Ryckman's 1931 winner. Even its title, "The Gentleman from Nebraska," is tongue-in-cheek. From a conservative Republican newspaper, the editorial was—depending on whose interpretation you accept—either an attack on Nebraska's progressive Republican Senator George W. Norris or a poke at the paradoxical political behavior of the state's provincial voters. It is an attempt to explain humorously why Nebraska voters continued to send Norris to Congress when he seemed more interested in other parts of the world than in Nebraska. While Norris undertook such crusades as attempting to have the federal government sell electricity from federally built hydroelectric plants directly to consumers rather than to private electric companies and to prevent federal subversion of civil rights, Ryckman charged that he did little more for Nebraska than make himself objectionable to federal officials. Had controversy been the custom with the Pulitzer Prize announcements, the response to Ryckman's award would have been predictable. Liberals charged that his editorial was an underhanded, cruel, bad-tempered attack on Norris. Conservatives said it was a well-done explanation of the paradox of Nebraskans supporting the liberal Norris while their other political heroes were conservative. Nebraska's citizens thought it was an attempt to smear Norris and insult their intelligence.

SENATOR George W. Norris, never lacking a mandate from the people of Nebraska in the course he has pursued as a member of the United States senate, now returns to Washington doubly assured of the unquestioned approval of his state and its people.

The senatorial record of Mr. Norris, with all its ramifications, has been endorsed in as convincing a manner as anyone could wish. Many reasons have been advanced as to why such an endorsement should not be extended to him. The opposition to Norris has been conducted as ably and as thoroughly as any group of capable politicians could do the job. The candidacy of as fine a statesman as Nebraska ever produced has been presented to the state as an alternative to that of Mr. Norris, and has been rejected.

Acceptance of the situation is therefore a matter without choice. To continue the argument is to waste words. The opposition to Senator Norris has been so completely subdued and so thoroughly discredited that further jousting with the windmill is more quixotic than Quixote himself.

There is not even good reason for being disgruntled over the result. For the purpose of the Nebraska political situation, 70,000 people can't be wrong. The will of the state is seldom expressed in so tremendous a majority, and it must be taken not only as an endorsement of Mr. Norris but also as at least a temporary quietus upon his critics and opponents.

The state of Nebraska has elected Norris to the United States senate this year, as it has many times in the past, mainly because he is not wanted there. If his return to Washington causes discomfiture in official circles, the people of Nebraska will regard their votes as not having been cast in vain. They do not want farm relief or any other legislative benefits a senator might bring them; all they want is a chance to sit back and gloat.

Nebraska nurses an ingrowing grouch against America in general and eastern America in particular. The state expects nothing from the national government, which it regards as largely under eastern control, and asks nothing. It has lost interest in constructive participation in federal affairs, and its people are in a vindictive frame of mind.

This grouch is cultural as much as political. Nebraska and its people have been the butt of eastern jokesters so long they are embittered. Every major federal project of the last half century has been disadvantageous to them. The building of the Panama canal imposed a discriminatory rate burden upon them. Various reclamation projects have increased agricultural competition. Federal tariff policies increase the cost of living in Nebraska without material benefit to Nebraska producers.

Nebraska voters have long since ceased to look to Washington for relief, and they no longer select their congressional representatives with relief in view. Neither George Norris nor any of his Nebraska colleagues in congress have been able to combat this hopeless situation. If Norris were forced to rely upon what he has done in congress for Nebraska, he would approach an election day with fear in his heart.

But Senator Norris has found another way to serve Nebraska. By making himself objectionable to federal administrators without regard to political complexion and to eastern interests of every kind, he has afforded Nebraskans a chance to vent their wrath. He is perhaps unwittingly, an instrument of revenge.

The people of Nebraska would not listen to George Norris long enough to let him tell them how to elect a dog catcher in the smallest village in the state, but they have been sending him to the senate so long it is a habit. If he lives long enough and does not get tired of the job, he will spend more years in the upper house of congress than any man before him. Death, ill health or personal disinclination—one of these may some day drive him out of the senate, but the people of Nebraska never will!

The state asks little of him in return. It gives him perfect freedom of movement and of opinion. It holds him to no party or platform. It requires no promises of him, no pledges. He need have no concern for his constituency, is under no obligation to people or to politicians. He can devote as much of his time as he likes to the Muscle Shoals power site, and none at all to western Nebraska irrigation projects. He can vote for the low tariff demanded by cane sugar producers of Cuba, while the beet sugar growers of Nebraska are starving to death. He can interest himself in political scandals in Pennsylvania, and be wholly unconcerned over the economic plight of the Nebraska farmer.

He can do all these things, and be as assured of election as the seashore is of the tide. He could spend a campaign year in Europe, and beat a George Washington in a republican primary and an Abraham Lincoln in a general election.

And yet, George Norris is not a political power in Nebraska. The people of other states believe he is revered as an idol in his own state. As a matter of fact, he is probably held in lower esteem in Nebraska than in any other state in the union.

His endorsement of another candidate is of no real value. He could not throw a hatful of votes over any political fence in the state. He gave his tacit support to La Follette as a third party presidential candidate in 1924, and the Wisconsin senator could have carried all his Nebraska votes in his hip pocket without a bulge. He came into Nebraska in 1928 with a fanfare of democratic trumpets and of radio hook-ups, stumped the state for Governor Smith—and Nebraska gave Herbert Hoover the largest majority, on a basis of percentage, of all the states in the union.

As far as the people of Nebraska are concerned George Norris is as deep as the Atlantic ocean in Washington, and as shallow as the Platte river in his own state.

The explanation of this fascinating political paradox is to be found not in an analysis of Norris, but of Nebraska. As a senator, Norris has given Nebraska something the state never had before. He has put the "Gentleman from Nebraska" on every front page in America, and has kept him there. A resident of Nebraska can pick up the latest edition of a New York daily or of an Arizona weekly, and find "Norris of Nebraska" in at least three type faces.

But the publicity Norris gets for Nebraska is not the whole story. His real strength in Nebraska is measured by the antagonisms he stirs up beyond the borders of the state. His people take delight in setting him on the heels of the ruling powers, whether of government, of finance or of industry. The more he makes himself obnoxious to a political party, to a national administration or to Wall street, the better they like him.

Nebraska is not interested in the smallest degree in what progress he makes, or what he accomplishes. It has been said of Norris that he has cast more negative votes against winning causes and more affirmative votes for lost causes than any other man in the senate. But every time he succeeds in pestering his prey until it turns around and snarls back at him, the chuckles can be heard all the way from Council Bluffs to Scottsbluff.

The summary of it all is that Nebraska derives a great deal of pleasure out of shoving George Norris down the great American throat. He has been an effective emetic in republican and democratic administrations alike, has worried every president from Taft to Hoover. His retirement from the senate, whether voluntary or forced, would be welcomed in more quarters than that of any of his colleagues.

The people of Nebraska know this, and enjoy it. Every time Norris baits the power trust or lambasts the social lobby, Nebraska gets the same amusement out of his antics that a small boy gets out of siccing a dog on an alley cat. When he shies a brickbat at a president, Nebraska has as much fun as a kid pushing over an outhouse.

You have to know the isolation of the hinterland to understand why this is so. Nebraska has sent many men to the senate who were more capable than Norris, as his predecessors and as his contemporaries. It has had other senators who have done more for the state and for the nation than he has.

But it has never had another senator who let the whole world know there was a "Gentleman from Nebraska" in the manner he has succeeded in doing. Nebraska could send a succession of great men and good men to the senate, and the east and west and south would never know there was a state of Nebraska or that such a state was represented in the senate. But Norris lets them know there is a Nebraska, and Nebraska does not care how he does it.

There is an instinctive resentment in the hearts of these people of the states between the Mississippi and the mountains against the failure of the far east to understand and appreciate the middle west. It crops up in politics, in religion, even in sports.

Nebraska is one of the richest of all the agricultural states and yet the wealth of its industries exceeds that of its farms. It has given such names as Gutzon Borglum, Willa Cather, John J. Pershing, William G. Dawes, William Jennings Bryan and a hundred others of prominence to the nation. It has unsurpassed schools, progressive cities and towns, people of intelligence and culture.

And yet the rest of the nation persists in regarding Nebraska as provincial, its people as backward. If the east thinks of Nebraska at all, it is as a state still in a frontier period. The national conception of a Nebraskan is that of a big hayshaker, with a pitchfork in his hands, a straw in his mouth, a musical comedy goatee on his chin, a patch on the seat of his overalls and the muck of the barnyard on his boots.

Nebraska has resented these indignities, but has given up hope of avoiding them. Its only hope is to pay back in kind. In the days of the real frontier, it vented its wrath on the occasional luckless tenderfoot from the east. Now it sends George Norris to the senate.

Norris does not represent Nebraska politics. He is the personification of a Nebraska protest against the intellectual aloofness of the east. A vote for Norris is cast into the ballot box with all the venom of a snowball thrown at a silk hat. The spirit that puts him over is vindictive, retaliatory. Another senator might get federal projects, administrative favor, post offices and pork barrel plunder for Nebraska, but the state is contemptuous of these. For nearly two decades Norris has kept Nebraska beyond the pale of federal favor, but his people consider him worth the price.

George Norris is the burr Nebraska delights in putting under the eastern saddle. He is the reprisal for all the jokes of vaudevillists, the caricatures of cartoonists and the jibes of humorists that have come out of the east in the last quarter of a century.

Too Much Government

(MARCH 25, 1932)

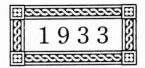

(for a series on national and international topics)

HENRY J. HASKELL
Kansas City (Mo.) *Star*

THE *Kansas City Star* won the 1933 Pulitzer for 19 editorials by
its editor, Henry Haskell. The editorials composed three series:
economic and political conditions in Europe, economic conditions in America, and the growth of government. The Pulitzer
jury praised Haskell's work as "a compelling demonstration of
editorial responsibility and leadership." Haskell, the jury said,
"pointed out the need for national economy and cited specific
cases where efficiency could be maintained in government at a
lower cost to the taxpayer. [He] commented clearly and in-
formatively on foreign developments without being sectionally
selfish." This editorial in the series on "Too Much Government" decries the growth of government bureaucracy, which
Haskell argues was aimed solely at serving itself rather than
the public. Though he sees the problem as grave, Haskell still
is able to retain a sense of humor. He wonders, for example,
how earlier American homemakers were able to make lemon
pies without government instruction. In another editorial dated
March 30 he points out that the growth of bureaucracy included
the establishment of a federal bureau of efficiency. Writing
from a conservative stance, however, Haskell faces the dilemma of deploring big government while accepting the fact
that government must "aid and encourage" economic groups.
Where to draw the line, therefore, between necessary and unnecessary government is a major point of focus for Haskell.
Though our public debate faces the same quandary, Haskell's
editorials of natural consequence now seem dated. In an
editorial of April 1 he laments the immensity of taxes and the
national budget. The totality of the former for all levels of
government was $13 billion annually in 1932; the latter was $4
billion. What would Haskell have hollered if he had known
Roosevelt's New Deal was just around the corner?

THE facts about the multiplying functions and agencies of the department of agriculture, laid before the house economy committee by Secretary Hyde, furnish another example of overproduction in government. The secretary has done well to recommend to congress that a number of these functions and agencies be abolished or turned over to the states.

The growth and expansion of the services supplied by this department are out of all proportion to the need or demand for them. They represent the aspirations of government rather than the needs of agriculture, which is true of all other departments. It is an evitable phenomenon of bureaucracy, which propagates itself, growing by what it feeds on.

The importance of the great agricultural industry of the United States cannot be overestimated; the propriety and necessity of the government to aid and encourage it never has been called in question. So well established is this principle, indeed, that it has become the convenient and unsuspected cloak behind which bureaucracy has chosen to operate. To aid agriculture, a market news service was established. That was proper and legitimate; but it is not proper and legitimate that this service should have been expanded until there are sixty-nine such market news service offices scattered throughout the country. The service itself is for agriculture; the operation of the service is in the interest of bureaucracy. It is proper and legitimate that the department should have field stations and laboratories for the benefit of agriculture; it is not proper nor legitimate that it should have 775 such stations, doing duplicate work. The expansion was not for agriculture, but for bureaucracy.

Agriculture, like all other business and industry, can best be served by a vigorous trimming of government. The country is being smothered by government services. It is being kissed to death. Many of these services are altogether unnecessary, others are a duplication of those furnished by the states and others, and, if they are proper at all, should be supplied wholly by the states. Some of them, indeed, should not be furnished by either the federal government or by the states, but by the homes, if they are required at all. In that class of services may be lumped all those by which government now seeks to instruct the American housewife in how to make lemon pies and rompers. How those problems were met by the wives and mothers of America before the department of agriculture was established, a little more than sixty years ago, nobody now knows, but in some way the Civil War was carried on and the western wilderness and deserts subdued without the bureau of home economics.

In reducing government to a size where it can be put into the clothes provided for it by the Constitution, congress should observe the simple rule that government is the servant of the people of the United States and not their master. Its function is to serve the people and not itself. When it gets out of bounds, as it now is, and assumes to build itself up for its own benefit at the cost of the people whose welfare it is supposed to promote, it should be put back in its place and with no gentle hand.

Where Is Our Money?

(DECEMBER 2, 1933)

EDWIN P. CHASE
Atlantic (Iowa) *News-Telegraph*

LIKE at least two earlier winners, Edwin P. Chase's prize-winning editorial was greeted with criticism. Written during the Great Depression when great numbers of people were out of work and banks were idle, the editorial is an attempt to explain the causes of the troubles. Reactionary and evidencing a conservatism typical of newspapers of the day, it is basically an attack on Franklin Roosevelt's approach of remedying the problems through government programs. Though its sentiments were out of touch with the desires of the majority of the public, the editorial was picked up by a number of the nation's leading newspapers. Criticism of the editorial's selection for the Pulitzer Prize came mainly from liberals, who chided Chase's piece for shallow, faulty reasoning and poor writing. In defense of the editorial, it might be said that it was a good attempt at providing an understandable analysis of an abstract, complicated problem. Stylistically, though the editorial is punctuated with rather crude phrasing, its satire and its strength of feeling are occasionally effective.

IT is announced that at 10 o'clock tonight, Iowa time, William Randolph Hearst, well known publisher, will broadcast an address on the subject which appears at the caption of this article.

The subject is a broad one and permits of many ramifications. Likewise the query is a live one and has been for several years with many people who formerly were in comparative affluence and have found themselves suddenly in a position where money is a scarce article. The whereabouts of the money of the individual is perhaps beside the point in this comment, if we stick to the text, as doubtless Mr. Hearst's broadcast will deal with the whereabouts of the funds of the nation as a whole, rather than the financial plight of the individual citizen; but the subject intrigues one and suggests a line of thought relative to the part the individual has played in rendering himself particularly susceptible to the injuries inflicted by the period of economic stress.

Where is our money? Here in Iowa, if competent statistics are to be

43

believed, during the ultra-prosperous years of the world war period when money flowed like water into the coffers of the farmer and the business man and everyone else, some 200 million dollars of good Iowa money went for stocks, shares in half-mythical concerns which were worth exactly their value as a piece of printed paper. During that period and shortly thereafter a good many hundreds of millions from the middle-west went into the first and second mortgage bonds of apartment hotels and the like, security issued on appraisals inflated to the nth degree. The most of these bonds are now worth just what the stocks we referred to are worth—the value of the paper and the printing contained therein. There is no way of estimating how many hundreds of millions of money the country over went up in smoke and vanished in thin air when it suddenly dawned on us that even the most productive land in a section like ours is not worth $300 or $400 an acre. It took only the simplest mathematics to arrive at that conclusion, for even at the prices brought by farm products at their peak, the return on the land in this section would not pay interest on an investment of $300 or $400 an acre. It can easily be recalled that during that hectic period it was considered a mark of provincialism not to buy a new automobile every year. A lot of fur coats and a lot of diamonds and a lot of expensive clothes for both men and women were indulged in by all classes. The wage earner suddenly awoke to the fact that by buying on the installment plan he could keep up with the Joneses and he not only spent every cent he could get his hands on in many instances, but he pledged the major portion of his wages or salary months ahead to pay for automobiles and other articles which were worn out by the time he had completed the payments.

These are but a few instances, cases in point. One might go on indefinitely telling of the wild orgy of spending and of contracting obligations without thought of the pay day and with little or no thought of the economic soundness of such spending. Then came deflation. We got down to cases. We danced and are still paying the fiddler. Like children we have sought someone to blame for our plight and also like children we now seek some magic way to cure our ills and expect the government to provide the cure. The man who contracted debts does not want to pay them just now, because in some instances, he cannot pay them. In every way we have met the crisis which was thrust upon us as though we had nothing to do with producing it. As a matter of fact, we had all to do with producing it. In the proportion that the individual citizen went haywire with extravagance and reckless spending governmental units went on the same kind of an orgy and whooped our taxes 100 per cent in ten years. Bond issues were pyramided by communities with the same disregard of the coming of the pay day which characterized the individual. We built great cathedrals of education, with motion pictures and swimming pools and all sorts of gewgaws and frills. We erected public buildings in many cases entirely beyond possible needs of communities for a hundred years. Just as private enterprise overbuilt in every direction, governmental building activities got out of bounds. The people have to pay the bill. The saturnalia of expenditure created fixed taxes, and taxes have a habit of certainty in good times and bad times alike. With our incomes and our business revenues depleted our tax bill in the main has remained the same. All an echo of the period of extravagance and wild-eyed inflation which brought about our troubles. We were talking about "two cars in every garage and a chicken in every pot," and we made much about the so-called American standard of living, whatever that meant. We insisted that all the various elements of our population should attain that standard, and we instilled into the minds of many people who could not afford it a desire for the things had by others more fortunate in life. Oodles of people who had no more business with an automobile than a wagon has with five wheels bought cars. Oodles of people learned to live beyond their means. It began to look as if it would not be long until there would be no one to do the work of the country, as all were seeking the same mythical standard to which we referred. And we still have the automobiles.

The bottom went out of things. Or it might be more appropriate to say that the top was blown off. Then the people of the United States commenced to take stock. Seeking someone to blame they listened to the fulminations of the politicians who represented the "outs" and who told that the way to cure their ills was to convert the outs into the "ins" and the ins into the outs. This they did, with their usual disregard of essentials and fundamentals. It became a pleasing fiction to attribute our plight to the tariff, and later to our money standard. The people were told that all that was necessary was to reduce the tariff which protects American manufacture and agriculture, and all would be jake. Now they are being told that the way to put money into the hands of those who are penniless, and make it possible for the debtor to pay his obligations and start things moving on a normal basis is to cheapen our money. A lot of other experimental schemes are being worked out by an administration of which the people demand action. We are spending huge sums of money, borrowed for the purpose, in an endeavor to squander ourselves back to prosperity. In the face of the fact that debt is one of the basic causes of our troubles, we are following the theory that incurring more debt would cure us. And in the face of the fact that excessive taxation is another of the causes of our trouble we are laying the groundwork for more of the same, under the delusion that the application of all of these methods will relieve us of the trouble which we brought on ourselves, aided and abetted by worldwide economic upheaval.

We are a queer lot, we Americans. We expect whichever party happens to be in charge of the government to so manipulate the handling of public affairs as to afford us a cure for the results of our own folly. We seem to assume that it is possible for us to get well economically by the waving of some magic wand. We think we can force prosperity, and to the majority of the people of the country prosperity means a return to the hectic days preceding the stock market crash of 1929. This theory disregards the fact that those hectic days were created by false and inflated values which in turn were created by a false and inflated philosophy. In the creating of this inflation we disregard all natural laws of economics, so it is but natural for us to expect to cure the trouble by the same process. But it cannot be done.

The only way back to solid ground and to a degree of prosperity and well-being commensurate with common sense and economic soundness will be by the application of thrift and hard work and the balancing of the budget of every individual. The old haywire days are gone forever. But a large percentage of our population still believes in Santa Claus and good fairies. The cause of the present economic condition of the country in large measure can be ascertained by every citizen by looking in the mirror. Each one of us contributed his share. There is nothing new about all of this. It has been the history of things in the world since the earliest dawn of civilization. Particularly has it characterized every postwar period. Humanity never learns. We have not progressed so far in our thinking, after all.

Where is our money? The answer is not difficult. It can be told in one short sentence. We spent it.

Bankrupt

(APRIL 18, 1935)

┌─────────────────────┐
│ **1936** │
└─────────────────────┘

(for distinguished editorial writing)

FELIX MORLEY
Washington Post

FELIX MORLEY submitted 34 editorials for his Pulitzer entry in 1936. Such a bundle of writings covered almost any subject imaginable, from Christmas to the trial of Bruno Hauptman for kidnaping the Lindbergh baby to the Supreme Court to taxes to politics to world affairs. Most of the editorials on the last subject dealt with the League of Nations and the growing threat of Adolph Hitler and Benito Mussolini. His editorial entitled "Bankrupt" is a criticism of what Morley calls the "bankruptcy of European statesmanship" and what he sees as the hypocrisy of League members in condemning Hitler's tactics. Apparent in the editorial is the opposition of conservative American politicians to the League. While their rejection of United States participation in the League undermined the organization from the beginning, they had no compunction about criticizing its failure. Morley conveniently and, it might seem, blindly ignores this fact. Senator William Borah was in such agreement with the editorial that he had it placed in the *Congressional Record*. On the positive side, it can be said that the editorial does attempt to give an analytical overview of why League actions were unsuccessful.

IN a sanctimonious resolution, which carries little hope for any fundamental improvement in the European situation, the Council of the League of Nations has formally rebuked Germany for her recent denunciation of the disarmament sections of the Treaty of Versailles.

The wording of the resolution, which declares that "Germany has failed in the duty which lies upon all members of the international community to respect undertakings which they have contracted," will make it virtually impossible for the German government to resume its membership in the League. But the action taken at Geneva yesterday does more than block that desirable step. It also calls for the development of a policy of economic and financial sanctions "which might be applied should, in

47

the future, a state, whether a member of the League of Nations or not, endanger peace by unilateral repudiation of its international obligations."

This, in effect, means the development of a definite anti-German alliance under the leadership of the victors in the last war. It is a tragic confirmation of the criticism of those who have maintained that the chief function of the League has always been to enforce the terms of the Versailles Treaty. It is a step toward surrounding Germany with a ring of steel which may, because of German economic weakness, for the present preserve an uneasy absence of actual hostilities. But it is the direct opposite of that policy of constructive statesmanship which would have sought to build real peace on a freely admitted equality of national rights.

Of course, the brutal, headstrong character of the Nazi government has invited this resolution at Geneva. But few of the nations which have so piously condemned the German action of March 16 are in a position to throw stones effectively. Six countries which have defaulted on their war-debt agreements with the United States solemnly approved the resolution's statement that "it is an essential principle of the law of nations that no power can liberate itself from the engagements of a treaty nor modify the stipulations thereof unless with the consent of the other contracting parties."

One of the Council members denouncing Germany in this lofty language was Russia, which has always maintained that obligations of the Czarist regime are not binding on its present government. Another condemnatory vote came from Poland, which less than a year ago unilaterally repudiated her obligations to the League in respect to minorities in her territory. Yet another rebuke to Germany came from Turkey, which shortly after the war pointed the way to Germany by forceful overthrow of the Treaty of Sevres. Italy, so scrupulous with respect to the treaty rights of Abyssinia—a fellow member of the League—is also prominent in the parade of the Geneva Pharisees. In fact, only Denmark, with a clean record on treaty observances, dissociated herself from the denunciation of the German kettle by other European pots.

The refusal of the victorious powers to regard Germany as an equal was primarily responsible for driving that country into the hands of the fanatics who now control her destiny. Confronted with a situation for which they must share the responsibility before history, the only concession of the war victors is to gild their mailed fist with a veneer of self-conscious rectitude. Nor is it to be overlooked that this portentous resolution makes no distinction between the violation of negotiated and dictated treaties.

The bankruptcy of European statesmanship was never more apparent than in the approval given this sorry declaration by the Council of the League of Nations.

Censorship, You—and Us

(OCTOBER 11, 1935)

(for distinguished editorial writing)

GEORGE B. PARKER
Scripps-Howard Newspapers

GEORGE B. PARKER shared the 1936 Pulitzer with Felix Morley. This was the first of two times that there were two recipients of the editorial writing award. The official Pulitzer Collection at Columbia University does not contain Parker's exhibit. Like Morley, however, Parker apparently covered a wide range of topics, though he had a particular interest in freedom of the press. His most frequently cited editorial is "Censorship, You—and Us." It shows Parker's concern not only for freedom of the press but for how European events in the pre–World War II period affected the press. Parker especially attempts to explain to readers how censorship imposed by European governments could affect the reliability of newspaper reports and how readers should react to war news. Scripps-Howard is unable to locate the editorial in its archives. Thus, printed below are fragments of the editorial that have appeared in various publications. The fragments are incomplete, but hopefully they have been edited in a coherent manner.

WE want to talk to you frankly . . . [How should you feel about the validity of war news in your paper?] The answer is that you are right to be suspicious. By no means should you put complete confidence in foreign dispatches. Use salt whenever you feel it is needed.

All we can guarantee is plenty of diligence . . . reinforced by considerable experience with the tricks of censorship learned from the World War . . .

So we hope to guard against many of the things we fell for once. But don't expect too much. Be ready to make your own discounts and your own deductions . . . So we want to ask your help in a problem that must necessarily be yours as well as ours.

Censorship and war go together just as censorship and dictatorships do. A correspondent . . . is under wraps . . .

Propaganda is as much a part of war as are machine guns and airplanes. In many respects it is the most important part. By it, nations in conflict seek to build up sentiment at home and support around the world . . . So you may expect propaganda from many sources. Even on this side . . . there will be carefully hidden propaganda agencies working for this side and that . . .

Accordingly, the best we can do is to ask you to join us in being wary and to assure you that you can depend upon us to be just as cautious as it is possible to be . . .

This is no time for artlessness either on the part of newspapers or newspaper readers. We wish we were all-seeing, but we must agree with Mr. Dooley, who said:

"Newspapers are not perfect, and neither is the human race."

The Opposition
(NOVEMBER 6, 1936)

(for distinguished editorial writing)

JOHN W. OWENS
Baltimore Sun

THOUGH a number of editorials were submitted as John W. Owens's Pulitzer entry, members of the Pulitzer committee let it be known that his editorial, "The Opposition," had particularly influenced them in awarding him the 1937 prize. Written shortly after the Republicans' disastrous loss in the 1936 presidential election, the editorial is an analysis of why the GOP's fortunes had sunk so low. Within the structure of a political history of the party, the editorial argues that the GOP was suffering from "intellectual poverty" and an absence of any well-designed proposal to solve society's problems or provide political direction. Owens concludes that in 1936 the intellect of the Republican party had dived to its lowest ever. In addition to his writing as editor of the *Baltimore Sun,* Owens authored a number of articles on politics for various magazines and journals and was considered an astute observer of the political scene. It might be pointed out as a matter of coincidence that the Nicholas Murray Butler mentioned in the latter part of this editorial was the president of Columbia University, through which winners of the Pulitzer Prize are selected.

THE careful reader may have observed in the recent campaign one important fact which was not mentioned in public discussions. It is the fact that no spokesman of the Republican party made the front page in the regular run of things save Mr. Landon himself. Democratic leaders made the front page—Davis and Griffith and others. But there were no Republican successors to the Roots and the Hugheses of other Presidential years. Not a single sledge-hammer speech, of the sort that Hughes and Borah made in the campaign of 1928, appeared on the Republican side in the entire campaign of 1936. Not a single Republican speech deserved the front page. And this, we think, is a fact that needs the attention of those who are trying to understand the present and prepare for the future.

In part, this intellectual poverty of the Republican party may be described as a quirk of fate. For, in part, it is due to the rise of the descendants of the immigrant groups in New England and New York. It is nearly twenty years now since Al Smith became a major figure and his appearance signaled a political revolution. It signaled the increasing power in the Democratic party in the Northeast of leaders who spring from the loins of the party's rank and file. Mr. Roosevelt's patrician leadership in the last four years does not alter the essential fact. And, simultaneously, Smith's appearance as a major figure signaled the increasing supremacy of the Democratic party over the Republican party in the Northeast. Not only in New York but in Massachusetts, in Connecticut, in Rhode Island, even in Maine a new order was at work which brought to the seats of power the Watshies, the Parleys, the Laucygans, the Spellacys. Their individual fortunes varied, but their collective power was established.

Quite suddenly, as history goes, the breeding grounds of Republican intellect failed. The sons of the immigrants were defeating the sons of the Puritans, and the latter were turning from politics. Compare the intellectual quality of the Republican representation in the Senate from the Northeast when Hoover yielded to Roosevelt with that when Taft yielded to Wilson. Other forces were at work. Probably the materialism which always had been the teammate of the austere idealism of the Puritan had acquired excessive weight. But, in any event, there was the plain fact that scions of Puritan wealth and Puritan education were being defeated by the sons of immigrants, and New York and New England were failing as the breeding ground of Republican intellect. Anyone who saw the party leaders who met Mr. Landon at Buffalo on his first trip into the East could measure the collapse with his own eyes.

At the same time, logic was doing a similar work in the Middle West and the West. Those areas had provided more Presidents for the Republican party, but less intellect. They had, however, produced their Shermans and their Hannas and their Allisons and, in later years, their Dollivers and La Follettes and Borahs and Norrises. And these Republicans of the Middle West and the West, representing to a very large extent yeoman constituencies, were insisting with ever-increasing vehemence upon the extension to their constituencies of the paternalistic government to which their party was committed.

Borah and Norris and Hiram Johnson might now and again inveigh against the special privileges accorded powerful interests by their party, and might even vote against them. But their real interest has been in extending paternalism to the little fellow in their constituencies. Their passion was reserved for fights to give him the benefit of the Government's resources. They were not so much against the Hamiltonian idea as they were in favor of means to augment the trickling down from top to bottom of largess bestowed by the Federal Government. Most of them would fight ten times for "benefits" for their own people to the one time they fought against the whole system of special favors.

And along came Mr. Roosevelt in 1933 and gave them in the White House a benediction they never had been able to get from their own party. He, no more than they and no more than Mr. Hoover and the Old Guard, made a frontal attack upon the whole system of special privileges. The structure of monopoly was never safer than in the plans and projects of the New Deal. But, whereas Mr. Hoover and his Republican predecessors insisted upon rugged individualism for the little fellow, though they could stomach a veritable mountain of special favors indirectly given to the big fellow, Mr. Roosevelt sought to make the scheme universal. Everybody was to get some sort of bounty.

The result was that he appropriated what was left of the intellectual vitality of the Republican party. At the very moment that the collapse of the Northeast as the great breeding ground of Republican intellect was complete, Mr. Roosevelt met the demands of the secondary breeding ground of Republican intellect and thereby absorbed it. Norris, Borah, Hiram Johnson, La Follette, Abuzens and the other Republicans of force in the Middle West and the West supported him generally in the New Deal and in the 1936 campaign backed him openly or passively.

The news editors who thrust Republican speeches other than Mr. Landon's into the inside pages were simply giving mute testimony to a great historical fact. There was left in the country scarcely a Republican who had anything to say (and was willing to say it) which deserved a place on the front page of any important newspaper. And how did Mr. Landon meet the situation? In the worst possible way.

He had been given a party platform that was a creaking, lopsided omnibus of vote-buying dodges, often mutually contradictory. Immediately after the Cleveland convention it was bruited that Mr. Landon was cognizant of the weakness of his platform and intended in his acceptance speech and in a few speeches that would follow to give coherence and order and an enlightened direction to his party's policy. His acceptance speech failed to carry forward this purpose, but the first few of his speeches on tour seemed to lay the foundation for a structure of genuine political liberalism. The parochial counselors overcame him. When he got down to specific issues, he was offering special favors to this group of States and that group of citizens.

The man who had spoken strongly and intelligently at Portland for liberalism committed himself at Des Moines, at Minneapolis and at Indianapolis to the sorriest schemes of reckless and extravagant paternalism, of sectionalism, of nationalism and of isolationism. By the time he was through, his own position was a hodge-podge of Old Guardism and New Dealism. His personal position was a reflection of the ramshackle platform given him at Cleveland.

Intellectual opposition to Mr. Roosevelt from the Republican party had simply ceased to exist. There was no semblance of any central idea of government in the Republican campaign. The campaign consisted in stimulation of ultra-conservative and reactionary fervors, on the one hand, and extension of New Deal bounties on the other. It closed as an amalgam of the worst features of Hooverism and of Rooseveltism.

Three brilliant and able young men had resigned from the Roosevelt Administration on issues which involved principle. They were Douglas, Acheson and Warburg. They wished to fight Mr. Roosevelt on questions of principle. Moreover, the circumstances attending their departure had been such that, as human beings, they craved the opportunity to fight. But when Mr. Landon had passed from the general to the particular in those speeches at Des Moines, Minneapolis and Indianapolis, those three men divided very much as the millions of the voters in the country divided. Warburg and Acheson made their way back into the Democratic camp. They found Mr. Landon accepting and even extending much that was worst in the Roosevelt regime and opposing that which they believed to be good. Douglas went through a mental struggle of weeks before he could decide that the balance still lay against Mr. Roosevelt.

In the small group that was left of the old intellectuals among the Republicans of the Northeast, there was almost unanimous silence. Perhaps it may be said that Mr. Root's great age barred him from participation in the campaign. But there is his spiritual son, Henry L. Stimson, the last Republican Secretary of State. He was not in the Republican campaign. And there is Nicholas Murray Butler, whose traditional Republican conservatism has given place in these days of violent nationalism to consistent preaching of the essentials of historic liberalism. He was not in the Republican campaign. For that matter, John Davis, the Democratic bolter who had the clearest understanding of Mr. Roosevelt's departure from Democratic liberalism, contented himself with an indictment of the President and avoided endorsement of the Republican candidate.

It is this intellectual collapse of the Republican party that, to those who have some understanding of the need of a two-party system in democratic government, is the worst feature of the recent campaign. Those who look superficially at the figures in the election totals may conclude that the opposition to Mr. Roosevelt has been reduced numerically to negligible proportions. Actually, the change of one voter in ten would lift the opposition to a very dangerous level. There would be no serious difficulty in building a formidable opposition to Mr. Roosevelt, and in thus preserving the two-party system in effectual form, if there were intelligence in the leadership of the Republican party. But the bald and unvarnished fact is that the intellect of the Republican party is at the lowest ebb in its entire history.

It follows, of course, that whatever opposition Mr. Roosevelt may invite as his policies are disclosed must come from the Democratic party, as was the case in 1933. And, if evoked, this opposition will have influence in 1937 as it had in 1933. But obviously the opposition of a Carter Glass must fall of its full force if the natural political opposition to Mr. Roosevelt can do no more than wallow in a sea of confused expediencies. If the Republican opposition is so stupid that it cannot understand why Carter Glass's opposition to New Dealism does not mean Carter Glass's support of Old Guardism, then Carter Glass may expect to fight a lonely fight. If the Republican opposition is so stupid that it cannot understand a fight on principle against Mr. Roosevelt's paternalism, if it is so stupid that it can only conceive a fight against wholesale paternalism in terms of a fight for paternalism in the interest of a few, then, indeed, is the outlook poor.

Which means that the responsibility of the historic liberal, the historic Democrat, is all the greater if and when Mr. Roosevelt shows the whites of his eyes in specific issues, as he did not do at any time in the campaign that gave him 523 electoral votes out of 581.

Tenancy Problem Is National
(NOVEMBER 27, 1936)

(for distinguished editorial writing)

WILLIAM WESLEY WAYMACK
Des Moines Register and Tribune

THOUGH the Pulitzer Prize administration does not have a file of the work for which William Wesley Waymack received the 1938 award, it is believed his editorials dealt primarily with growing farm tenancy in the United States in the 1930s. L. W. McGuire, former promotion manager for the *Des Moines Register and Tribune,* said he thought "Waymack came to the attention of the Pulitzer judges with a series of articles on farm tenancy written late in 1936 and entered in 1937. Apparently the judges were waiting for the entry the next year and gave him the prize." Waymack's entry, McGuire added, probably covered a "wide range of subjects," including, in addition to farm problems, political issues, civil liberties, international affairs and industrial relations. The *Register and Tribune*'s Pulitzer Prize file contains articles on farm tenancy written by Waymack in 1936. These, assumes Don Benson, director of public events for the paper, "were among those submitted on Waymack's behalf for the Pulitzer Prize." In the editorial below, Waymack argues that tenancy was not simply a regional or farm problem but that it was national. Showing an understanding of the implications tenancy had for the future of the country, he calls for national awareness and action to eliminate it.

IT is announced that regional hearings will be held between the first and the middle of next month by the president's committee on farm tenancy—two meetings in the south, two in the middle west and one on the west coast. The one on the west coast is in a sense supplementary.

These regional hearings, which are intended to bring out every possible point of view or proposal that thoughtful individuals or groups may be nursing, tend to emphasize the regional phase of the tenancy problem.

And there are regional differences, sharp and significant ones.

There is by no means an adequate understanding as yet between the several sections most vitally affected. Not even among our more well-informed people. We in the cornbelt know too little about the special aspects and urgencies of the problem in the cotton south, and they of the cotton south are deficient in acquaintance with cornbelt conditions.

Yet the big thing to get in mind, as we begin for the first time to face the problems of conserving our soil and creating or conserving a high type of rural population, is that the problem is basically national, not sectional.

In its long run effects, if we are to remain a united country with freedom of movement for both goods and people between the sections, the broad problem of land tenancy is indivisible.

It is true that conditions in the deep south are infinitely worse than they have become in our part of the country.

There, thanks to the Civil War, the race question, a vicious system of one-crop, cash-crop production, and other factors, we have a population of millions of low grade farm tenants.

They have a high birth rate. They include vast numbers of Negroes, but a larger number of whites. Many of them are thoroughly incompetent, though they may come from the purest American stock. They exist far below the level of European peasants, who at least have homes, a reasonable degree of security, and a wholesome way of life.

Some millions of these southern tenants are in reality not tenants at all. They have no capital. They own no stock or equipment. They are wage slaves on the farm, working year after year to catch up with current debts to merchants and others and never catching up. Their houses are often shanties, lacking windows or cook-stoves. They know nothing of modern sanitation. They have practically no educational opportunity. By various devices they are often disfranchised—by cumulative poll taxes, for instance.

Of course the soil has suffered, soil not so good as ours in any case.

Of course the existence of such conditions has begun to produce bitterness and radicalism.

That, drawn starkly, is the ugliness of the situation in parts of the south.

Now, does any sane man think that conditions of that sort can go on forever without somehow affecting us?

The future population of our cities is going to be drawn largely from these southern low-castes. Our citizenry of tomorrow is in their seed.

The squeezing out of both Negroes and whites, who move north to compete not only with our industrial workers but also with our farm renters, tends inevitably to lower standards both in our cities and on our farms. Already in southern Iowa there has been some influx of renters from the south. This accentuates the yearly shifting of tenants. It accentuates the mining of soil. It accentuates the lowering of human values. Father Ligutti of the Granger Homestead enterprise has pointedly referred to one phase of it as the "importation of illiteracy."

Moreover, there are other very specific economic ways in which south and north are inseparable.

Merely as one illustration, let us consider the matter of foreign markets for the south's cash crops. If our national tariff or other policies should result in permanent loss of any large part of our European and Japanese cotton markets, millions of acres of cotton land would inevitably go into other production in competition with the cornbelt, including the crops of which we already tend to have annual surpluses for export.

There are great regional differences with respect to the farm tenancy problem, as we said in the beginning.

In the south there is the enormous social task of somehow reversing the degenerative tendencies of generations, of starting to build the lower levels of the population up to the point at which a sound rural civilization is even possible. That—we may as well face it—is probably going to call for some species of governmental paternalism that we should prefer not to engage in.

In the cornbelt we have more fertile land and more competent people. We have the handicaps of a speculative tradition that are extremely difficult to counteract. And we have leasing practices that no longer fit our type of agriculture and that run contrary to the public interest.

We have an "agricultural ladder" that used to enable people to climb from farm laborer to farm renter to farm owner, but which in recent years has worked in reverse—it has given us farm owners descending to tenants, farm tenants descending to lower levels of tenancy, and the lower levels descending to farm labor.

But the main thing is that the problem as a whole is a distinctly national problem.

The degree of emphasis on different phases of such solutions as the country may adopt will vary in different sections.

But it is vital to each affected section that solutions be found in all sections.

We are members one of another. There is no escaping that.

My Country 'Tis of Thee . . .

(OCTOBER 2, 1938)

(for distinguished editorial writing)

RONALD G. CALLVERT
Portland Oregonian

As the world became slowly entangled in the tragedies that led to World War II, the American press—as it had done during the era of the first global war—again took on a cloak of patriotism. The war theme dominated the Pulitzer Prize for Editorial Writing. A presage of things to come in the prizes was Ronald Callvert's 1939 winner, a patriotic song of America. Like few other editorials, it is blatantly lyrical, an effect gained by its repetition of the phrase "in this land of ours, this America." As luck would have it, Callvert wrote the editorial because another writer was unavailable. When he thought of the idea, Callvert said, "it occurred to me as a good editorial for Ben Hur Lampman to write." Lampman was noted for his lightness of touch as an *Oregonian* editorialist. The editorial was criticized for inanity and superficiality, but it quickly drew the attention of readers, especially churches, schools, and patriotic organizations. To meet the demand for reprints, the *Oregonian* issued the editorial in leaflet form and distributed more than 14,000 copies. Though the Pulitzer was awarded to Callvert for general editorial writing during the year, judges pointed out "My Country 'Tis of Thee . . ." as exemplary of his work.

In this land of ours, this America, the man we choose as leader dons at no time uniform or insignia to denote his constitutional position as Commander in Chief of armed forces. No member of his Cabinet, no civil subordinate, ever attires himself in garments significant of military power.

In this land of ours, this America, the average citizen sees so little of the army that he has not learned to distinguish between a major and a lieutenant from his shoulder straps. When the Chief Executive addresses his fellow-countrymen they gather about him within handclasp distance. Goose-stepping regiments are not paraded before him. When he speaks to the civilian population it is not over rank upon rank of helmeted heads.

59

In this land of ours, this America, there is no tramp of military boots to entertain the visiting statesman. There is no effort to affright him with display of mobile cannon or of facility for mass production of aerial bombers.

In this land of ours, this America, there is no fortification along the several thousand miles of the northern border. In the great fresh water seas that partly separate it from another dominion no naval craft plies the waters. Along its southern border there are no forts, no show of martial strength.

In this land of ours, this America, no youth is conscripted to labor on device of defense; military training he may take or leave at option. There is no armed force consistent with a policy of aggression. The navy is built against no menace from the Western Hemisphere, but wholly for defense against that which may threaten from Europe or Asia.

In this land of ours, this America, one-third of the population is foreign born or native born of foreign or mixed parentage. Our numerous "minorities" come from fourteen nations. The native born, whatever his descent, has all political and other rights possessed by him who traces his ancestry to the founding fathers. The foreign born of races that are assimilable are admitted to all these privileges if they want them. We have "minorities" but no minority problem.

In this land of ours, this America, the common citizen may criticize without restraint the policies of his government or the aims of the Chief Executive. He may vote as his judgment or his conscience advises and not as a ruler dictates.

In this land of ours, this America, our songs are dedicated to love and romance, the blue of the night, sails in the sunset, and not to might or to a martyrdom to political cause. Our national anthem has martial words; difficult air. But if you want to hear the organ roll give the people its companion—"America . . . of thee I sing." In lighter patriotism we are nationally cosmopolitan. Unitedly we sing of Dixie or of Ioway, where the tall corn grows, of Springtime in the Rockies, or of California, here I come.

In this land of ours, this America, there is not a bomb-proof shelter, and a gas mask is a curiosity. It is not needed that we teach our children where to run when deathhawks darken the sky.

In this land of ours, this America, our troubles present or prospective come from within—come from our own mistakes, and injure us alone. Our pledges of peace toward our neighbors are stronger than ruler's promise or written treaty. We guarantee them by devoting our resources, greater than the resources of any other nation, to upbuilding the industries of peace. We strut no armed might that could be ours. We cause no nation in our half of the world to fear us. None does fear us, nor arm against us.

In this land of ours, this America, we have illuminated the true road to permanent peace. But that is not the sole moral sought herein to be drawn. Rather it is that the blessings of liberty and equality and peace that have been herein recounted are possessed nowhere in the same measure in Europe or Asia and wane or disappear as one nears or enters a land of dictatorship of whatever brand. This liberty, this equality, this peace, are imbedded in the American form of government. We shall ever retain them if foreign isms that would dig them out and destroy them are barred from our shores. If you cherish this liberty, this equality, this peace that is peace material and peace spiritual—then defend with all your might the American ideal of government.

Europe's Emperor

(MARCH 17, 1939)

(for distinguished editorial writing)

BART HOWARD
St. Louis Post-Dispatch

BART HOWARD was known for his skill at capturing a situation with a phrase and for the sparkle of his writing. He was especially fond of graphic description and alliteration. These characteristics are apparent in one of the editorials included in Howard's entry for the 1940 prize, "After the Battle," a comment on politics inspired by the overthrow of Thomas Pendergast's machine in Kansas City. "Corruption," the editorial philosophized, "is a spineless creature. Bossism, which personifies corruption, has no sinew, no fiber, no stamina. It may be a big, brazen braggart, as the Pendergast machine was, but the minute it is challenged by a Governor with fight in his eye, the minute the people see that the issue has been joined and swing into formation—that minute the Pendergast machine's finish was 'in the bag.'. . . We have seen the state-shadowing Pendergast machine crack, crumble and collapse in the gale of a resolute public opinion. The machine's hangers-on will scatter like chaff in the wind." More than for his talent, however, Howard surpassed other editorial writers because, said a fellow staffer on the *St. Louis Post-Dispatch,* of his sincerity, his "deep and abiding convictions," and a "great faith in the dignity of the individual and in the validity of democracy." Howard's editorials submitted for the Pulitzer Prize had no common theme, but the editorial below—analyzing Adolph Hitler's conquests—is typical of his work. It makes apparent his use of language and is prophetic in its vision.

THE massive memory of Bismarck shrivels in the blazing sun of Adolf Hitler's conquests. The former won by "blood and iron," utilizing intrigue as a preface. The latter wins by strategy of conference, fortified by force, to be sure, and punctuated by the threat of marching armies.

Schuschnigg is summoned to Berchtesgaden for an afternoon in the torture chamber, and Austria is expunged from the map while Vienna becomes Berlin's scrubwoman.

How many a plotting hour ticked secretly across the clock as Hitler suggested and Henlein acquiesced may only be surmised. But at last the Sudeten Germans, under superb coaching, were letter-perfect in their parts, and the Reich was ready to rescue their brothers from the tyranny of "ruthless Czecho-Slovakia." What would the neighbors say—the great Powers pledged to safeguard that one green isle of democracy in stormy Central Europe? France was explicitly committed; Russia conditionally; England impliedly. Chamberlain made his pilgrimage to the Fuehrer's mountain retreat, and later, with Daladier, consented to the pillage of the little Republic at Munich's midnight.

With Austria and the Sudetenland securely possessed and the plunder respectably approved, Herr Hitler's hunger was satisfied, rapacity was foresworn, there would be no more raids in Europe. "The Sudetenland," said Hitler at the Berlin Sportspalast on September 26, 1938, "is the last territorial demand I have to make in Europe." And in an earlier September speech at Nuremberg, he said he had given the guaranty to Chamberlain: "We do not want any Czechs any more."

England believed, officially. So did France. Russia refused to be deceived, distrusting Hitler's vow and subsequently impugning the motives of both Chamberlain and Daladier. Russia's suspicions have been frightfully vindicated, and today London and Paris join with Moscow in pronouncing worthless the word of Hitler. And Mussolini's Rome, at the other end of the paper axis, sees in the once barred doors of the Brenner Pass an open gateway for a Colossus in growing pains.

In Dr. Tiso of Slovakia, Hitler seems to have found a craftier confederate than Henlein of the shriekingly managed Sudeten affair. Or perhaps Der Fuehrer has acquired a more polished technique. Surely the consummate skill of this latest coup, that caught the world flat-footed, may not be denied. Machiavelli could write it. Hitler does it. The revolt of Slovakia, inspired, promoted and directed in Berlin, is a masterpiece of statecraft. Moralists may deplore. Lights may burn late in sleepless chancelleries. The thing is done. A *fait accompli,* in the language of diplomacy, and the architect of the German Empire awakes in the historic castle of centuries-old Prague to breakfast contentedly and to count his gains.

He counts his gains realistically. Slovakia's independence lived but a day. Tiso, the politician, may now turn back to the priestly beads he seemingly had forsaken. The swastika is his country's flag.

What a vulturous Ides of March for the ravished, murdered homeland which Masaryk's genius had guided into the stature of a fine nation! The swastika flies over Bohemia and Moravia, and Hungary comes up from the south to seize Carpatho-Ukraine, with Poland ghoulishly hurrying to the feast of death.

The German Empire, territorially, is mighty today, and Hitler has inventoried the spoils with barbaric gusto.

The continental balance of power, deftly maintained, with grave lapses, of course, by Britain's ministerial jugglery, trembles under the tread of Europe's Emperor.

Toward Totalitarianism

(FEBRUARY 11, 1940)

(for distinguished editorial writing)

REUBEN MAURY
New York Daily News

WHILE many of the Pulitzer Prize editorials, and perhaps most of the recent ones, are thoughtfully reasoned but typically written, a few are shallow in thinking but facile in wording. Reuben Maury's editorials are examples of the latter. Maury received the 1941 award for six editorials:

—"Chemistry—The New Frontier" (January 3, 1940), a review of technical advances during the preceding decade and a speculation of things to come;
—A three-part editorial (January 27) endorsing a drive to save the Metropolitan Opera, discussing the presidential election and urging continuation of work relief;
—"Satellite Nations" (March 24), an expression of doubt that small nations could continue to exist independent of a large, aggressive neighbor;
—"Moses' Crosstown Highway Plan" (May 26), an approval of a plan to erect three elevated highways across Manhattan;
—"Anti-Semitism in This Country" (September 24), an argument against the belief that Jews were pushing the United States into World War II.
—"Toward Totalitarianism," reprinted below.

The editorials generally are marked by a superficiality of thought and written in an interesting, simple manner aimed at a huge mass audience, reminiscent of the techniques of Arthur Brisbane, former editorialist for the Hearst newspapers. Critics greeted the announcement of Maury's award with charges that he was a "self-confessed hireling" who wrote for two publications of differing political views and that his editorials were irresponsible. In the editorial reprinted here, Maury argues that policies of Roosevelt's New Deal, especially those regulating business, were moving America "toward totalitarianism."

WE often get the feeling in these wartime days that a strong current in human affairs is running somewhere, but that we can only guess from chips on the surface whither the current is going.

We think the best guess is that it is setting toward totalitarianism all over the world—meaning toward state control of the individual and of business.

Russia and Germany have arrived at complete totalitarianism; Italy has the forms of it; General Franco's Government in Spain is heading toward a "vertical syndicalist" state which reads like totalitarianism to us.

Even more significant to a person trying to dope out world trends, Great Britain has gone a long way toward totalitarianism since the war began last September. When the government begins to tell people to douse their lights, send their children to the country, and how much meat they can eat, that is state control of the individual where he lives. Now that this control has been clamped on Englishmen, we doubt that it ever will be fully relaxed.

As soon as the war broke out, France put civil liberties on the shelf for the duration—outlawed the Communist Party, began arresting people for saying so much as a kind word for Hitler, and so on.

The United States is on the road toward totalitarianism, though whether we'll eventually go the whole route is another question.

Time was in this country when business, any business, was practically a free agent.

Those big, expansive, devil-take-the-hindmost days began coming to an end in 1887, when Congress set up the Interstate Commerce Commission to curb some of the predatory habits of some of the railroads. Social control after social control has been fastened on business and the individual in this country since then—income, inheritance and gift taxes, soft coal commissions and workmen's compensation boards and Indian Welfare bureaus, labor relations acts and the Wage-Hour Law, etc., etc., etc., and a few more etc.'s.

Under the impetus of the New Deal, we've gone a longer way toward totalitarianism in seven years than we went in the previous 20 years. By the same token, the European war is taking Britain and France toward totalitarianism much faster than they would have gone had the horrors of peace continued to afflict them. Wars hurry economic changes along, every time.

We think the history of Europe since 1914 adds support to our theory that the world is headed toward totalitarianism.

The World War tossed into the ash can the thrones of three great empires—Germany, Austria-Hungary, Russia—along with the idea that some people are born to lord it over a lot of people who are born to be lorded over.

This war is rapidly taking away money and property from those who have a lot of those things—conscription of securities in England, confiscation of the Thyssen fortune in Germany, savage income taxes everywhere.

Life under totalitarianism is apparently not as pleasant for most people as life in a democracy. But neither, we should think, is it unbearable.

For one thing, the New Deal's government controls had to happen if there wasn't to be an attempt at revolution in this country against concentration of too much wealth in too few hands. It was evolution that brought those things to us, not a malevolent Mr. Roosevelt determined to smash up the Hooverian paradise of 1929–33.

For another thing, everybody who has a job is more or less caged anyway; there's no such thing as perfect freedom.

We do hope, though, that if the United States goes in for totalitarianism some way can be found to preserve the freedom of the mind. We mean freedom of speech and press, liberty to say what you think, whether your thoughts are worth a hoot or not. A system under which we had not only to live and do business as the Government ordered but also had—as in Russia and Germany—to think as the Government thought, would be unendurable, we believe, to most Americans.

The Urgent Need of Unity

(JANUARY 15, 1941)

(for distinguished editorial writing)

GEOFFREY PARSONS

New York Herald Tribune

As events leading to World War II burned hotter in Europe in 1941, Americans still faced domestic disagreements. In a series of 17 editorials, Geoffrey Parsons issued a "plea for unity" in the *New York Herald Tribune*. Coming from a Republican paper, the editorials called for Republicans to put aside partisanship and for Republicans and Democrats to unite for the common good. In nominating Parsons for the Pulitzer award, the journalism jury pointed out the integrity of Parsons's editorial stance. "This series by the chief editorial writer of a leading Republican newspaper," the jury stated, "urges national unity behind the national leader whom this editorial writer and his paper had vigorously opposed for re-election and whose domestic policies Mr. Parsons still asserts leave much to be desired. These editorials seem outstanding examples of cooperation in a crisis by an opposition newspaper, are carefully reasoned, contain scholarly background, and are vigorously expressed in excellent and calmly persuasive prose." In announcing the award of the Pulitzer to Parsons, the Columbia University trustees added this citation: "The selection of these editorials over others of great distinction and to the same patriotic purpose was chiefly influenced by a wish to recognize an outstanding instance where political affiliation was completely subordinated to the national welfare and a newspaper firmly led its party to higher grounds." The first editorial from Parsons's series follows.

THAT the nation is face to face with the gravest crisis since the Civil War hardly admits of dispute. Within the next few months—perhaps within two months, perhaps within six—there seems certain to be decided the tremendous issue, whether this country will face Germany and the future with allies or without them. If the latter, then our children and our children's children are all too likely to live in a world at war, perpetually arming for military combat, in economics endlessly struggling against totalitarian controls. To say that our national standard of living may be put back fifty years by such a world-wide warfare is certainly not to exaggerate.

Before such a crisis the need of national unity grows hourly. We do not mean a unity artificially imposed by law or threat or social pressure. We mean a unity achieved through frank debate, respect for disagreement and a realization that personalities and partisanship have no place in such an hour.

It is a matter for sincere regret that the President still refuses to take the lead in bringing about such a spirit of union. That he should have consulted the opposition in Congress before the submission of the lease-lend bill is now generally conceded. That that bill contains no provision for keeping both sides of the Houses informed as to steps taken under the tremendous grants of power contained in it, is equally a matter for regret. Passage of the bill could have been expedited and sources of friction and disunity avoided had Mr. Roosevelt approached the problem from a broader outlook, with partisanship forgot.

But the opposition will only make an unfortunate situation worse if it responds in kind. Now, if ever, Republican statesmanship has a chance to demonstrate its capacity by placing the patriotic needs of the time above personal irritations or factional disputes. We ask Republicans to be generous toward one another in this period of stress and that all who debate the issues, of whatever party, hold the national purpose clearly before them in all they say and do.

This is not to suggest that debate be slighted or hurried decisions reached. We trust that ample discussion will be insisted upon and that the excesses of the bill will be relentlessly lopped off. Similarly, in the more general debate in the nation at large there must be the fullest opportunity for every side to be heard—those who oppose any aid to Britain as well as those who believe that full aid to Britain is essential to American defense.

But it is possible to conduct such a debate without personal recriminations and with the hope and resolve to seek out the common wisdom of the American people. The time calls, above all else, for open minds, clear thinking and fair, generous discussion. There should be no petty questioning of motives, no substitution of epithet for reason.

For one important thing, let us be sure of our facts. For this reason we think Mr. Wilkie is rendering an important public service by undertaking the risks of a first-hand study of the English problem. For another, let us as far as possible, abandon catch phrases and formulae that no longer apply. For another, let us summon all our national gifts of imagination that we may see the issues not only for the immediate present but for the long future.

This newspaper believes firmly that aid to Britain is the only possible means to avoid war. It also believes that the issue of peace and war does not and has not for a considerable time been within our power to control or decide. The leader of Germany will or will not make war upon us as the coldest of military calculations determine; and if he decides upon war he will fix the moment by the same relentless logic. And, whether he decides to war upon us in a military sense or not, a long and vastly more destructive economic warfare is inevitable unless we should yield and become, like France and the small democracies, in an economic sense, a slave nation.

But we welcome the contrary views of our readers, and we shall, as always, be glad to give them full voice in our columns. We ask only that debate be about realities and that, in view of the gravity and urgency of the crisis, the discussion be kept upon a high plane of good will and patriotic endeavor. The goal is "Unity"; only in such a spirit and by such ideals can it be achieved in time.

Statesmanship in the Legion
(MAY 3, 1942)

(for editorials published during 1942)

FORREST W. SEYMOUR
Des Moines Register and Tribune

FORREST SEYMOUR became the fifth winner of the Pulitzer for editorials inspired by World War II. His entry was composed of 23 editorials covering generally three themes: the home front, bringing about an intelligent peace, and making democracy work. Most of the editorials deal specifically with aspects of the war, but they also cover such topics as politics, the national economy, and the poll tax. The editorial receiving most attention, "Statesmanship in the Legion," applauds the American Legion's adoption of a resolution favoring an antiisolationist role for the United States when World War II should end and the Legion's recognition that the United States must assume a role of leadership to assure world order. The editorial also received the American Legion Editorial Appreciation award for 1943.

IN the *Register*'s opinion, the statement about America's role in the world ahead that was adopted by the national executive committee of the American Legion Friday is one of the notable contributions of our time to statesmanlike public leadership.

The Legion does exercise an important leadership. Though occasionally during its quarter century of life we have disagreed with one or another of its policies, its influence on the whole has been excellent. We have frequently said this. Especially during the last ten years, after the disasters that international suspicion and disunity were breeding had become apparent, the voices of national Legion leaders began to be heard more and more frequently on the side of intelligent recognition of this nation's world responsibilities. More than one of these leaders, incidentally, were Iowans.

Since the Legion is quite representative of the whole American people, it has naturally gone through the same period of debate in this epoch that all of us have. But because it has been essentially progressive and attuned by its very character to popular sentiment, it has been "out ahead" of many comparable forces in its recognition of the political realities and its shift to practical and courageous policies.

Now, through its national executive committee, it has "gone to bat" for the principle upon which all of our long-run hopes for a decent future world hinge. That part of the committee's statement which sums up this principle is worth repeating. Here it is:

It was considered that what the last war proved and what this war emphasizes is:

That, whether we like it or not, we are a part of the entire world; that as a nation we cannot escape repercussions from mighty social, economic and political upheavals in any quarter of the world; that isolationism is dead; that now is the time to condition the public mind for full acceptance of this inexorable fact.

That, however complete the military victory may be, we cannot win the peace, we cannot provide assurances to our people against periodic repetition of our involvement in world catastrophes, unless we as a major nation recognize and assume our responsibilities and take our position of leadership in organizing the world to establish and maintain order; that there can be no assurance of permanent national security except through world security.

That says it all, and says it magnificently.

We would call attention to two or three other things with respect to this.

First, the Legion took this stand by approving the report of its coordinating committee, which had been consulting with spokesmen for a half dozen other national groups exerting a similar wide influence among their respective memberships. They were the National Grange, the American Federation of Labor, the National Association of Manufacturers, the Elks, the Knights of Columbus, B'nai B'rith, and the Masonic lodge of New York.

This sort of consultation among large national associations exercising a broad influence and leadership is certainly nothing to be sneezed at. We do not know how it got started. But it is a grand thing. We assume that it will continue to develop.

Second, this statement of principle was hinged, naturally and properly, on an acknowledgement that winning the war has to come first.

That goes without saying.

The wisdom that is being displayed in America, by committing ourselves to intelligent participation in the postwar organization of the world, does not need to detract a whit from the energy with which we fight for the essential military victory. On the contrary, the prospect of wise and informed leadership after the war will give point to our sacrifices, and permit more zealous concentration on the job at hand.

More than that, the faith and valiance of all the harassed and suppressed peoples of the world—both our existing and potential allies—depend in large measure on our clear understanding of what they are struggling for and of our own urgent place in the world's future.

The Legion by its nature is a symbol of the best of military experience and valor, combined with the best of civilian leadership and statesmanship.

It is no small matter, as we see it, that this organization's strength and influence are plainly going to be exerted in the years ahead on the side of intelligent world order.

How Germany Fooled the World
and
That Valley Falls Latin Teacher

(for editorials written during 1943)

HENRY J. HASKELL
Kansas City (Mo.) *Star*

HENRY HASKELL is the only person who has received the Pulitzer award twice. For his second prize, Haskell submitted as his entry seven complete editorial pages from the *Kansas City Star,* of which he was editor. While the editorials covered a wide range of topics such as education, politics and Social Security, the predominant subject was World War II and related international problems. Reprinted here are two editorials from the February 28, 1943, editorial page. "How Germany Fooled the World" recites a history lesson to support Haskell's analysis of why the Treaty of Versailles ending World War I was unsuccessful. It urges that similar "mistakes" be avoided when World War II should end and that strong measures be imposed on postwar Germany. "That Valley Falls Latin Teacher" criticizes attempts by the National Education Association to use the war as an excuse for eliminating cultural studies from high schools.

HOW GERMANY FOOLED THE WORLD
(FEBRUARY 28, 1943)

THE Commission to Study the Organization of Peace has just made its third report. Other committees and groups are busy with the same studies. We are constantly and properly reminded that unless we are both intelligent and vigilant we may win the war only to lose the peace. Whether any generally accepted plan is worked out or not, all this discussion is to the good. The problems of the post-war world are as formidable as those of the war itself.

It was the American Patrick Henry who said: "I know of no way of judging the future but by the past." At this time it is important to survey what happened after the first World War in order to avoid the mistakes made in that fateful period.

Some of the discussion of the new world order has a familiar ring to those whose memories go back to the other war—the kaiser's war, just as this is supposed to be Hitler's war.

We keep hearing that whatever is done about Germany, the German war criminals must be punished; the officers, that is, who ordered the shooting of hostages, who were responsible for the vast and ghastly atrocities against Poles and Jews, who ordered the bombing of Rotterdam and the machine-gunning of refugees on the roads of France, who planned the destruction of Lidice.

After the war, it is agreed, Germany must be disarmed and an army of occupation maintained on German soil. Then some sort of a world authority must be set up; something comparable to the League of Nations, but with more power to keep the peace. In all these plans we are cautioned to bear in mind that the German people were not responsible for Hitler and the war. At the last free election for the Reichstag Hitler's party received only a minority of the vote. The Germans are like every other civilized people. All they really desire is to live comfortably at home in peace. They were dragged into an unwanted war by a paranoiac dictator who had established his rule by intimidation and the Gestapo, so the argument runs.

The idea of punishing the war criminals is not new, but probably few Americans recall that such punishment was included in the Treaty of Versailles. The kaiser was to have been punished, but he was out of reach in Holland. Evidence, however, had been collected in the cases of 900 lesser men, and under the treaty Germany agreed to hand them over to an Inter-Allied tribunal for trial and punishment.

But unexpected difficulties developed. A cry of protest to the civilized world went up from Germany. Such procedure would be an intolerable insult to a great nation. The new German democratic government appealed to the Allies not to burden it with the odium that would attach to any government that attempted to carry out this provision of the treaty. The French were obdurate, but liberals elsewhere turned a sympathetic ear to the plea. After all why humiliate a proud people needlessly? The Weimar republic offered to have the criminals publicly tried by the German supreme court at Leipzig. The British government yielded and the French could not hold out against it. The preliminary proceedings took a year. Finally twelve of the 900 were tried, and six convicted. The British solicitor general asserted in the House of Commons that the trials were "a new milestone in the course of international justice." The official

English observer at the trials, Sir Ernest Pollock, declared that while they might not have fulfilled the expectation of the public "they were of real importance and value. They had made history." And that was that.

Naturally the victims of German aggression were determined after the last war that Germany should be completely disarmed, just as they are today. The army was to be reduced to 100,000 men and there was to be no general staff. An Inter-Allied Control commission was set up under a French general with an English general as second in command. It was at work for several years. There were disagreements as to the size of the army. The English general took the position that the private armies with which Germany abounded were to be considered as part of the Reichswehr. When Hitler came to power it was estimated that the army included 250,000 highly trained troops instead of the 100,000 permitted by the treaty. A general staff was set up under another name. The republic's minister of defense confided to his friends that he would establish the general staff as the Institute of Textile Studies, if necessary.

There was complaint that word was always received two days in advance of the visits of the commission and that machine tools and supplies mysteriously disappeared. German airplane factories were set up on friendly Russian soil and a submarine plant established on the Spanish coast, so that experimental work could be carried on.

When Germany was admitted to the League of Nations in 1926 it was necessary that the control commission issue a final report that the disarmament provisions had been complied with. The report was made and suppressed by the democracies anxious to get Germany into the League. Later General John H. Morgan, adjutant general of the commission, wrote: "Germany has never disarmed, has never had the intention of disarming, and for seven years has done everything in her power to hinder, deceive, and countercontrol the commission appointed to control her disarmament."

At Versailles the French had contended that disarmament was not enough. Foch had insisted on the Rhine as a natural defense and he had urged the setting up of an autonomous Rhineland as a buffer state. He was overruled, but all the Allies agreed that Allied forces should occupy at least part of the Rhineland until 1935. In the conference Clemenceau said: "In fifteen years I shall be no more. In fifteen years, if you do me the honor of visiting my grave you will be able to say, I am sure, 'We are watching on the Rhine and we shall remain there.'"

But in 1929 as a gesture of appeasement and good will Briand consented to the withdrawal of all Allied troops, with the Rhineland itself remaining a demilitarized zone. Seven years later the Reichswehr marched in and France again was under the guns. The British government, and liberals everywhere said this was only natural. Any nation of course would insist on the right to do what it chose within its own territory, and Hitler's move was no threat to world peace.

When Germany entered the League of Nations in 1926 there was universal rejoicing and a general feeling that the millenium was at hand. But within a few years national dissensions paralyzed the League and it proved helpless to stop aggression anywhere. Even when Germany withdrew and openly threw off the mask of disarmament, nothing was done.

In retrospect it is evident that all the policies adopted to make Germany a peaceful, good neighbor were vitiated by one fundamental mistake. That mistake was the assumption that a peace-loving German nation had been forced into war against its will by a wicked government. Germany did not change with the flight of the kaiser. The ideals of a militaristic Germany able to dominate by force persisted under the republic as they had under the empire. What Mirabeau said more than a century ago was still true. Germany was "not a country with an army, but an army with a country."

The mistakes of the post-war years are obvious. How to avoid similar mistakes in the future involves problems of immense difficulty. But certainly we must build on a foundation free from the fundamental error that followed the last war. At Versailles under the idealistic leadership of President Wilson the assumption prevailed that the German people were misrepresented by their government; that once the government was changed, they could be trusted. In the light of the evidence we must assume that Hitler is right in saying that he speaks for the mass of the German people. An entire nation must be deprived of its power to do harm until it is re-educated in the essentials of civilization. Our post-war measures must be framed with this fact steadily in mind.

THAT VALLEY FALLS LATIN TEACHER
(FEBRUARY 28, 1943)

THE campaign of the National Education association to take advantage of the war to drive out cultural studies from high schools has evoked wide protest. One of the replies to the association's pamphlet on the subject comes from Justice William S. Smith of the Kansas Supreme court. The association took the ground that the teaching of ancient languages and literatures should be confined to "the very few" who might be expected to use them "in their scholarly pursuits," or whose cultural life might be enriched by them.

Justice Smith inquires how a high school teacher is to determine which students would achieve sufficient cultural value from Latin and Greek to warrant their studying these languages. The justice adds: "I was fortunate enough to come under the tutelage of a dear little old maid who loved to teach Latin in the Valley Falls high school. Under her influence I studied Caesar and Cicero and read the Aeneid twice. At that time my experience in Valley Falls constituted my entire cultural life. I have thanked the memory of that schoolteacher many, many times."

The advocates of the purely practical education would turn out a generation of trained cooks and machinists—which is all very well, for our civilization needs them. But they would smother the cultural life, which is destructive of civilization itself.

It would be a drab world if the National Education Association succeeded in banishing from American high schools the Valley Falls teachers who love the classics and in keeping from the Bill Smiths of the future that contact with the past that helps to an understanding of the present.

Relations of Freedoms

(DATE UNCERTAIN)

1945

(for editorials, especially on freedom of the press)

GEORGE W. POTTER

Providence (R.I.) *Journal-Bulletin*

GEORGE POTTER'S winning entry consisted of a number of editorials dealing with various aspects of World War II, but the
Pulitzer jury made especial note of his editorials on freedom of
the press, covering such subjects as wartime censorship.
These, the jury said, "expressed accurately and pertinently the
American view of freedom of the press." Special attention was
called to one editorial, "Relations of Freedoms," dealing with
the importance of a sound economic base for the press. The
system of income through advertising used by the American
press, Potter argues, is what guarantees press freedom. Without this or some such system independent of the government,
he says, the press cannot be free of influence by the government or corrupt private interests since it would have to rely on
one or the other for its financial support. While this theme is
constructed in the first half of the editorial, Potter in the latter
part switches emphasis to the importance of private property.
Thus the editorial, economically conservative, is as much a defense of private property as of press freedom.

IN the proper spirit of nonpartisanship, both Republicans and Democrats
in Congress, using spadework material gathered by the State Department, are uniting on a resolution to guarantee world freedom of news.
The aim is to incorporate in the peace treaties guarantees underwritten
by the signatory nations affording the right to gather news anywhere and
to permit the unhindered receipt into their countries of news gathered
elsewhere.

The premise of this resolution is so obvious that it does not require
laboring. It is that war, or the threat of war, is minimized and that better
relations prevail among the nations of the world when there is free access
to honest and unbiased news and information, objectively presented. We
know from bitter experience that the first thing that totalitarian [govern-
ments] and dictatorships do when they come into power is to seize the

press and make of it an instrument of totalitarian design to poison the minds of their people, color their thinking and stir up hatred and rancor against other nations. Through their control of the press, the totalitarian authorities effectively blanketed their people from information of or contact with the outside world.

But it is merely a counsel of perfection to suppose that there can be genuine world freedom of news without a genuine free press. A genuine free press is one that is economically free, that is, one that can support itself by its own revenues and stand on its own two feet independent of subsidy or subvention from government or self-seeking or selfish private interests. In France before the war, freedom of the press was guaranteed as a right, but in fact the French press was venal and corrupt because it was not economically free and depended upon subsidies and bribes for its bread and butter, often from foreign powers, with results that were calamitous to France. Pertinax, the most profound student of journalism in France, put his finger exactly upon the solution of how to get a genuine free press in that country: "The French people," he said, "will have to develop the advertising habit or be prepared to pay much more for their papers." In other words, the French press must be able to pay its own way in order to have real freedom, and that truth applies in any country that wants a free press.

Some people in this country do not understand or deliberately misinterpret what freedom of the press actually is. They father the idea that it is a right belonging to newspapers solely, giving them the privilege of doing as they please. As a matter of fact, freedom of the press is a specific grant of a right by the Constitution not to the newspapers solely but to all the people for their protection. We have the freest press in the whole world, thanks not alone to a jealously guarded popular right but also because the American press is economically independent, stands on its own two feet without subsidy or subvention and can pay its own way, depending upon its own competency for survival. Through our co-operative system of newsgathering, which serves newspapers of all shades of opinion, the American people are assured of objective news.

Thus we see in the instance of the American press a definite and inextricable relationship between a flourishing human freedom and the sound fruits of a healthy economic freedom. One depends upon the other, and both will prevail so long as conditions are maintained which permit this economic freedom.

Does the individual in America see clearly that his human freedoms are tied in with economic freedom?

There is a well-known generalization that human rights come before property rights. It is used by demagogues, because of its surface appeal, to play upon the emotions of the unthinking. Like all glib generalizations it should be subject to critical examination. We would not say that property rights come before human rights or that human rights come before property rights. Unqualified absolutes like these do not contain the truth as tested by human experience. What we do say is that human rights and property rights are related to one another, are intertwined with one another, work with and play upon one another for the general good, depend upon one another.

Pope Pius, in a recent statement of most far-reaching significance for the reconstruction of the world, said this much better than we can hope to say it, said it out of [a] background of deep human experience for the guidance of the men who will help build the new world. He related private property, a "natural fruit of labor," to man's determination "to create for himself and his own an existence of just freedom, not only economic but also political, cultural and religious."

He condemned a capitalism that "arrogates unlimited right to property without any subordination to the common good," and he condemned a system that, depriving men of any direct or indirect security in their lives, leaves them slaves of any political party that promises them bread and security. "By defending private property," said the Pope, "the Church . . . also pursues a lofty ethical-social aim. . . . The aim of the Church is to render the institution of private ownership such as it should be in accordance with the plans of Divine wisdom and the dictates of Nature: one of the elements of the social order, a necessary premise of human initiative, an impulse of labor for the advantage of the temporary and transcendental aims of the goal, the prize and dignity of man, who was created in the image of God. . . . Future social and economic-policy organizing activity of the State, of local bodies, of professional organizations will not be able to achieve their lofty aims in continuing the fruitfulness of the social life and normal returns of a national economy unless they respect and protect the vital function of private property in its personal and total value."

In other words, the Pope says that human rights and property rights, human freedom and economic freedom, are not antagonistic or divided into separate categories. They go hand in hand in a proper and related balance for the welfare of all. An understanding of this fundamental relationship will make for a better and more prosperous condition for us all.

Go For Broke
(AUGUST 27, 1945)

```
┌─────────────────────┐
│  1946               │
└─────────────────────┘
```

(for a series on racial, religious, and economic tolerance)

HODDING CARTER
Delta Democrat-Times (Greenville, Miss.)

AFTER serving in World War II on the *Stars and Stripes,* Hodding Carter returned to his newspaper in Greenville, Mississippi, and immediately began attracting nationwide attention. In numerous editorials he concentrated on building respect between races. For such writing he was awarded the 1946 Pulitzer Prize. "I had been protesting editorially against racial and religious injustices for a long time before our editorials won a Pulitzer Prize," he said. "But . . . the Pulitzer prize induced more people at home to concede that there might be some merit in what we were saying." After winning the Pulitzer, he was also known to have proposed tongue-in-cheek a new slogan for his small chicken enterprise: "All our pullets are prizes." The most popular editorial of his prize-winning series is "Go for Broke," written shortly after V-J Day. Though it is outwardly a challenge to white Americans to treat Japanese-Americans as equals, there is little doubt that Carter intended it to call for racial tolerance for blacks also. "Go For Broke" was widely reprinted and is one of the most frequently quoted Pulitzer Prize editorials in the history of the award.

COMPANY D of the 168th Regiment which is stationed in Leghorn, Italy, is composed altogether of white troops, some from the East, some from the South, some from the Midwest and West Coast.

Company D made an unusual promise earlier this month. The promise was in the form of a communication to their fellow Americans of the 442d Infantry Regiment and the 100th Infantry Battalion, whose motto is "Go For Broke," and it was subscribed to unanimously by the officers and men of Company D.

In brief, the communication pledged the help of Company D in convincing "the folks back home that you are fully deserving of all the privileges with which we ourselves are bestowed."

The soldiers to whom that promise was made are Japanese-Americans. In all of the United States Army, no troops have chalked up a better combat record. Their record is so good that these Nisei were selected by General Francis H. Oxx, commander of the military area in which they are stationed, to lead the final victory parade. So they marched, 3,000 strong, at the head of thousands of other Americans, their battle flag with three Presidential unit citationed streamers floating above them, their commander, a Wisconsin white colonel, leading them.

Some of those Nisei must have been thinking of the soul-shaking days of last October, when they spearheaded the attacks that opened the Vosges Mountain doorway to Strasbourg. Some of them were probably remembering how they, on another bloody day, had snatched the Thirty-Six Division's lost battalion of Texans from the encircling Germans. And many of them were bearing scars from those two engagements which alone had cost the Nisei boys from Hawaii and the West Coast 2,300 casualties.

Perhaps these yellow-skinned Americans, to whose Japanese kinsmen we have administered a terrific and long overdue defeat, were holding their heads a little higher because of the pledge of their white fellow-soldiers and fellow-Americans of Company D. Perhaps, when they gazed at their combat flag, the motto "Go For Broke" emblazoned thereon took on a different meaning. "Go For Broke" is the Hawaiian-Japanese slang expression for shooting the works in a dice game.

The loyal Nisei have shot the works. From the beginning of the war, they have been on trial, in and out of uniform, in army camps and relocation centers, as combat troops in Europe and as frontline interrogators, propagandists, and combat intelligence personnel in the Pacific where their capture meant prolonged and hideous torture. And even yet they have not satisfied their critics.

It is so easy for a dominant race to explain good or evil, patriotism or treachery, courage or cowardice in terms of skin color. So easy and so tragically wrong. Too many have committed that wrong against the loyal Nisei, who by the thousands have proved themselves good Americans, even while others of us, by our actions against them, have shown ourselves to be bad Americans. Nor is the end of this misconception in sight. Those Japanese-American soldiers who paraded at Leghorn in commemoration of the defeat of the nation from which their fathers came, will meet other enemies, other obstacles as forbidding as those of war. A lot of people will begin saying, as soon as these boys take off their uniforms, that "a Jap is a Jap," and the Nisei deserve no consideration. A majority won't say or believe this, but an active minority can have its way against an apathetic majority.

It seems to us that the Nisei slogan of "Go For Broke" could be adopted by all Americans of good will in the days ahead. We've got to shoot the works in a fight for tolerance. Those boys of Company D point the way. Japan's surrender will be signed aboard the Missouri and General MacArthur's part will be a symbolic "Show Me."

Apathetic and Pathetic

(MARCH 7, 1946)

(for distinguished editorial writing)

WILLIAM H. GRIMES
Wall Street Journal

OCCASIONAL Pulitzer-winning editorials seem to have struck a popular chord and gained wider currency than the columns of the parent newspaper. One such editorial is William H. Grimes's "Apathetic and Pathetic," one of 15 writings submitted as his 1947 Pulitzer entry. Most of his editorials dealt with economics, business or labor. This editorial includes references to these subjects, but it is more concerned with what Grimes saw as America's abandonment of its traditional values. Coming basically from a conservative point of view, Grimes, the *Journal*'s editor, criticized economic and political trends in the United States and the apparent contradiction in what Americans said they believed and in how they acted. The editorial was reprinted in a number of newspapers, and the *Journal* received more than 30,000 requests for reprints.

CONCERNING Premier Stalin's Russia and its international conduct, there are a great many puzzling aspects. To us the most puzzling is not rooted in Russia. It grows in America. It can be expressed in the form of a question: Why should anybody expect Stalin to do anything different than he is doing? If any surprise is due, it is in the fact that Stalin, being what he is and having the opportunity that he has, should be even as moderate as he has been.

The opportunity is that a ruthless man believing in the law of force has no opposition. And he has none because the only nation in the world around which could rally "a decent respect to the opinions of mankind" is losing its faith. It is becoming ashamed of its traditions. The light of freedom for the individual which has heartened men for a century and a half flickers and burns low in a fetid atmosphere from which the sustaining oxygen has been drained.

Try this if you will. Go into any group—the more prosperous and fashionable the better the test—and speak of the "self-evident truth" that "all men are endowed by their Creator with certain unalienable rights, that among these are life, liberty and the pursuit of happiness." Say to this group that "to secure these rights governments are instituted among men."

We venture that you will be startled by the number of people, particularly younger people, who do not know that you are quoting the Declaration of Independence. And of those who know, a large number will not agree with the philosophy expressed. And of those who agree— and this is the most tragic thing—many will not have the courage to say so.

Perhaps the dominant attitude was summed up by a young man who would probably think of himself as an "intellectual." He said:

"Only a few people in the Bible Belt believe those things now."

Or listen to the young minister of the gospel who came to this office sneering at those who "operate in a vacuum of idealism."

We gave our government encouragement—it did not need much— to connive with Stalin. In the criminal decision of Yalta an American President accepted secret agreements which bartered thousands of human beings and which, if carried out, will send thousands more to exile and death.

We did that and a chorus of writers and commentators defaulted their obligation to ask questions and said that Yalta was good. They said Stalin was a man of his word. He would not grab territory. He would not suppress the churches. He would cease to send his agitators into every corner of the world. He would not use his military power to force on other peoples his own social and political system. Each of those things he has done. Some illusionists, who said he would not, now have the decency to acknowledge disillusion. They suggest that we shake an admonitory finger at Stalin.

That is a ludicrous suggestion. Does anyone imagine that Stalin is such a fool that he thinks we can or will oppose his armed might with ours? And if we are not ready to do that, what other means of opposition have we? We have none, for we have besmirched our own moral precepts. We have dropped our faith and stand grotesquely naked.

Yet we tell other peoples of the world how they must act. We have abandoned the tradition that peoples have the right to work out their own destiny.

We denounce a Colonel Peron of Argentina as a dictator and a bad man suspected of aggression and therefore he must not rule that unhappy republic. He certainly is those things. But who is the United States to denounce the man that the people of his country apparently have chosen in a free election and to condemn any other government for cooperating with dictators? The fact is that Colonel Peron helped himself to power by borrowing more than one page from the book of the New Deal.

But Colonel Peron and General Franco, another unsavory character ruling Spain, are, we say, corrupt. Furthermore, they suppress the rights of the people. They poison the wells of free information. They certainly do those things.

Let us see what government it is that hurls these accusations of corruption and extralegal sanctions.

It is a government where the family and the friends of a President could use their prestige to enrich themselves and those who publicly protested are denounced. It is a government against which, for the first time in American history, Americans fear to speak. It is a government which is spending the people's money on a bureaucracy with which men abhor contact because resistance means reprisals. The system has the expected results. Many businesses feel that they must have a friend at court and so some who have official access are paid as "advisers." There was a time when we called such men lobbyists and investigated them. Now they are appointed to high office.

Looking at our record of connivance with dictators and looking at our domestic scene, is it any wonder that the people of Argentina decided that Colonel Peron might be the lesser of two evils?

And while we condemn the dictators for suppressing and distorting the free flow of information, our own State Department proposes a plan to blanket the world with propaganda.

Why should Stalin take us and our pious protestations seriously? Why should he give us any attention at all? He knows what is happening and he knows that we are treading the path to his philosophy and his orbit. He thinks he has only to wait—and he may be right.

We have told the world about four freedoms but the number of men who live under the heel of dictatorship is greater, not less. We have not stood for freedom. We are in the thick of the game of power politics. We are in it in Europe and in Asia and we have imported it to the American continent. It is Stalin's game and of course we do it badly.

There are men not afraid to speak out. One is John Foster Dulles who dares speak and knows whereof he speaks. We quote:

I am afraid we've got very few friends in the world today. There was a time when we had more friends than any other people of the world. Today we have influence because of our production capacity, because people are trying to get the physical things we produce. I don't detect any real friendship on the part of other peoples. This leaves us in a dangerous and vulnerable position; one which we should do our utmost to correct.

A man's standing in his community is a projection of his own character. A nation's standing in the world is a projection of its domestic life.

What we see at home is a condition where public trust is openly accepted as an avenue to private gain; where a government is so steeped in propaganda lies that it must give the wrong reasons for its policies; where in the name of freedom the citizen is being handcuffed to rules of a troupe of brilliant pygmies who write the prescription for a fuller life on an adding machine; where debt is prosperity and thrift a social crime; where it can be asserted that there exists a "moral right" to steal and bribe; where men shout free enterprise and then seek better and bigger government subsidies; where women leaving black markets stop to sign petitions for continuation of price control; where groups demanding "When do we get ours?" no longer whisper but shout and where officials no longer consider it necessary to conceal that they are the creatures of these groups.

Is it any wonder that in our international relations we cannot combat the assertion that black is white and that the goal of human freedom is the slave state?

Is it any wonder that Mr. Dulles laments the lack of those policies, "expressive of the righteous faith of the best in America?"

We are apathetic: We are rapidly growing pathetic.

We Will Not Be Intimidated

(MARCH 15, 1948)

(for distinguished editorial writing)

VIRGINIUS DABNEY
Richmond (Va.) *Times-Dispatch*

VIRGINIUS DABNEY, former editor of the *Richmond Times-Dispatch,* is one of those few writers who have received the Pulitzer Prize without submitting an entry. The Pulitzer committee, Dabney says, "decided to make the award to me on the basis of my work 'during the year' and with nothing before them." As a result, there is no file of Dabney's work for which he received the 1948 prize. Unsuccessful at selecting an editorial appropriate for inclusion in this anthology, Dabney says he is "unable to recall any 1947 editorial that is exceptional in any way." It is generally believed, though, that Dabney was awarded the Pulitzer for his stands on racial issues in the South. During the 1940s he was a staunch opponent of the poll tax and the one-party political system while favoring increased opportunities for blacks and equal though segregated facilities. His attitude toward editorial policy has been that writers must take stands on important local issues and not waste space on trite or irrelevant subjects. To improve the editorial page, Dabney wrote in a 1945 magazine article, the page "must be dedicated to the welfare of all the people, not merely to the interest of one exclusive and fortunate class. . . . More money will have to be spent on it, and more talent allotted to it. Then readers will turn to it in the expectation of being informed, stimulated, or amused, not in the confident knowledge that they will find there the same old sloppily written pontifications, the same dreary and bumbling half-truths, the same pachydermatous attempts at humor, where there is any humor. The effective editorial page . . . should be put together with some consideration for style, it must be vigorous, independent and free, and its judgments must have perspective, while permeating the whole there must be a passionate concern for the truth." Included here is the editorial for which Dabney won the 1948 Sigma Delta Chi award for editorial writing. A defense of freedom of the press, it makes evident the *Times-Dispatch*'s determination to oppose the

Virginia legislature's intention of investigating the newspaper. One of its primary persuasive appeals is its equating the state house of delegates with historic despots, while its apparent reasonableness on the issue of libel law moderates a stand that some readers might consider nothing more than self-serving.

THE Virginia House of Delegates has passed a resolution instructing the State Corporation Commission to investigate Richmond Newspapers, Inc. This absurd action was taken in retaliation for criticisms leveled at members of the General Assembly, and more particularly members of the House, during the session just ended.

The *Times-Dispatch* does not intend to be silenced by any such political skulduggery. This newspaper has spoken its mind freely during the recent session of the State Legislature, and it will continue to speak its mind. No threats from any section of the State, or from any branch of the General Assembly, nor yet from the Democratic machine, will influence its course.

The issue here is far bigger than the question [of] whether a Richmond newspaper should criticize the Virginia Legislature. One of the bulwarks of free peoples is involved.

George Mason's immortal Bill of Rights, which is a part of the Virginia Constitution, and has been virtually copied in the Constitution of the United States, as well as in the constitutions of the other 47 States, says (Article 1, Section 12, Virginia Constitution): "That the freedom of the press is one of the great bulwarks of liberty, and can never be restrained but by despotic governments."

The laws of libel, both criminal and civil, are always available, of course, to any citizen who is aggrieved by improper newspaper criticism.

There are all kinds of newspapers, just as there are all kinds of people, but once the freedom of newspapers or individuals to criticize public figures is hampered or curtailed, the first step toward dictatorship has been taken.

In country after country where the liberties of the people have been quenched, under Fascist, Nazi or Communist rule, one of the first steps has always been the smashing of the independent press.

The Second World Congress of the Communist International had this to say:

Only when the proletarian dictatorship has deprived the bourgeoisie of such powerful weapons as the press, the school, parliament, church, the government apparatus, etc., only when the final overthrow of the capitalist order will have become an evident fact—only then will all or almost all the workers enter the ranks of the Communist Party.

Adolf Hitler said in *Mein Kampf:*

It [the State] must not let itself be misled by the boast of a so-called 'freedom of the press,' and must not be persuaded to fail in its duty and to put before the nation the food that it needs and that is good for it; it must assure itself with ruthless determination of this means for educating the people.

Here in America there have been examples of interference with liberty of newspaper expression by officials or legislatures. One of the earliest occurred at the end of the eighteenth century, when the *Richmond Examiner,* a Jeffersonian organ, was attacked under the notorious Sedition Act for its political editorials. The effort to stifle the *Examiner* was unsuccessful.

The late Huey P. Long, as Governor of Louisiana, had his servile legislature impose a ruinous tax on all the Louisiana newspapers of large circulation because they had criticized his administration and exposed its rottenness. The tax was pronounced unconstitutional by the Supreme Court.

Frank Hague, the Jersey City boss, struck at the *Jersey Journal* by firing any county or city employee seen reading the paper, and by bringing about the withdrawal of certain advertising.

Similar techniques have been employed both in this and other countries. Those who employ them violate one of the principles on which American liberty has been founded, a principle for which oceans of blood have been spilled.

The resolution of the House of Delegates is a threatening gesture designed to arouse public prejudice. It is not motivated by ethical intent to correct economic injustice; its purpose is to gag the press.

So long as this newspaper is in the hands of its present ownership and management, it will not be gagged.

It will fight fiercely the concentration of governmental functions in a few hands, and the making of governmental policies by a small group of insiders.

It will not be muzzled, by the House of Delegates, or any other agency.

The *Times-Dispatch* will not be intimidated.

Imagine, One Billion!
(OCTOBER 1, 1948)

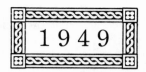

(for distinguished editorial writing)

JOHN H. CRIDER
Boston Herald

IN 1949, for the second time, the Pulitzer Prize for Editorial Writing was shared by two journalists. John Crider, editor of the *Boston Herald,* concentrated primarily on the 1948 presidential election in the editorials submitted as his Pulitzer entry. All the editorials were datelined outside Boston, although it is uncertain whether they were actually written from these places or in Boston. The *Herald*'s publisher, Robert Choate, in his cover letter with the entry, expressed his enthusiasm for datelined editorials. "The exhibit," he wrote, "is limited to [Crider's] out-of-town editorial writing because I believe it represents a novel and constructive departure from the conventional editorial style. . . . It does impress the reader with the editor's proximity to the news." Typical of the style and Crider's anti–Harry Truman leaning is the editorial below.

ABOARD PRESIDENT TRUMAN'S TRAIN, in Illinois, Sept. 30—President Truman said a most significant thing yesterday before his audience in the stadium at Tulsa. He said that for the first time in the history of Oklahoma its farm crop topped one billion dollars in value. There were some cheers and quite a bit of applause. "Imagine," he added, "one billion dollars."

Of course, this was just another attempt by the Democratic candidate to appeal to the native pride of the very proud Oklahomans. As a matter of fact, the $1,000,000,000 he mentioned would be around $600,000,000 or less if spoken in terms of 1939 purchasing power of the dollar.

But the funny part of it was that the President never mentioned "inflation," one of his favorite themes. In that Tulsa speech, it was mighty flattering to tell the Oklahomans they had produced such a crop.

He soon spoiled it, however, by adding that this huge production record was due in very large part to the farm policies of the late President Roosevelt which he had carried forward. He wouldn't let the people of Oklahoma rest in the belief that they had done something great themselves.

But worse, he didn't explain that the reason the produce income was so large was at least partly due to the inflated value of the dollar. Nor did he say that Oklahomans had to pay almost as much more than the value of their ordinary crops for what they bought from the East. Nor did he talk about what the President has tried to do to let union leaders run hog wild, as they say in this part of the country, with wage rates and monopoly control by deeply rooted union leaders.

That one billion dollar brag was the strange case of the loud-spoken anti-inflation President boasting about inflation. It is one of the strangest brags on record.

Church Unity
(AUGUST 29, 1948)

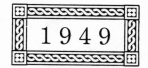

(for distinguished editorial writing)

HERBERT ELLISTON
Washington Post

HERBERT ELLISTON submitted 23 editorials as his entry for the Pulitzer Prize, the editorials covering a wide range of topics from politics to religion. Elliston was formerly on the staff of the *Christian Science Monitor,* and a number of his editorials reflect a particular interest in religion. "Church Unity" is typical of Elliston's approach. A commendation of the intent of the World Council of Churches to become a permanent organization, the editorial provides the opportunity for Elliston to express his hope that the action will help "restore vitality to religion." The editorial appears to reflect Elliston's personalized view of Christianity, but it is not clear exactly what his view is since the editorial tends to jump quickly from one subtheme to another. The primary problem with the editorial's style comes from Elliston's attempt to cover too many aspects of the major theme in such a short space. As a result, the editorial is disjointed and a number of ideas are presented without being adequately defined in the context of the editorial. We get a mention of Communism, an interchurch schism, religious form and content, philosophy, particularism and a number of other topics without ever being shown their particular relevance. Then we are left with the "hope that [the Council decision] will not degenerate into words signifying nothing" without being given any reason to suspect why such an unhappy result might occur.

ARNOLD TOYNBEE in his recent volume *Civilization on Trial* says that Western civilization has been "living on spiritual capital. Practice, unsupported by belief, is a wasting asset, as we have suddenly discovered, to our dismay, in this generation." This is a passage that John Foster Dulles quoted in his address to the World Council of Churches meeting at Amsterdam. Out of the conference came a decision which represents a great and worldwide effort to put enough belief into practice to restore vitality to religion. After ten years as a provisional body, the World Council, with 450 delegates representing 150 churches in 40 countries, has formally declared itself a permanent organization. There are big gaps even in this formidable nucleus of churches. The Roman Catholic Church, whose fold embraces the greatest number of Christians of any church, was not present, nor were the Russian Orthodox Church and the Southern Baptist Convention of the United States. But, if the new body falls a long way short of a reunion of Christendom, a historic event occurred, nevertheless, at Amsterdam. It "will go on working daily," as Mr. Dulles said, "to mobilize Christian power to break down the walls of division."

Clearly the fact that a pseudo-religion is on the march is the major event that has awakened the churches. Communism has flourished in a soil compounded of many elements. But one of them is undoubtedly the undermining of religious faith by the deepening and extension of schism and the deadening influence of mere ritual without works. This has diverted men to the worship of such false gods as nationalism, communism and fascism. It may be argued that extreme sectarianism has developed as a result of a series of rebellions against the elevation of form above content. If unity in diversity could have been maintained, the total effect would have been beneficial, but with splinteration has gone a dissension and a pride in theological dogma which fly in the face of Holy Writ. If the fatherhood of God is the fundamental belief of most of mankind, surely the corollary—the brotherhood of man—cannot be denied. The great gulf fixed between the two conceptions in the hearts and minds of most of the God-worshipping world is an abomination in the sight of God.

In this respect philosophy, which, according to Bertrand Russell, is something intermediate between theology and science, is coming to the support of religious belief, though organized religion fails to take advantage of it. The part is being rejected for the whole, and the only reality is the reality of relations—in the arts and sciences no less than in life itself. In other words, particularism of any kind has ceased to be acceptable on philosophical, let alone on religious, grounds. The time is thus overdue, in terms of the modern enlightenment no less than in those of the great challenge, when the whole armor of the church should be put to the task of restoring God in our daily life, lest Satan take possession of the vacuum. We hail the Amsterdam decision, and hope that it in turn will not degenerate into words signifying nothing.

First Things First

(FEBRUARY 20, 1949)

(for distinguished editorial writing)

CARL M. SAUNDERS
Jackson (Mich.) *Citizen Patriot*

WITH world tensions increasing in 1948, Carl M. Saunders, editor of the *Jackson Citizen Patriot,* and his clergyman asked one day over dinner what could be done. Strain between the United States and Russia was deepening. Saunders came up with the question and an answer, "Why don't we—all of us in America—pray for peace? We've tried rattling our tanks and planes; we've tried calling names; we've tried the United Nations. Let's put first things first—let's have a day of prayer for peace." He wrote an editorial pointing out that since Memorial Day is commemorated in honor of those who have died in war, no observance could be more appropriate than prayer that there be no more war. His suggestion caught on. A resolution was introduced into Congress, and President Harry Truman issued a proclamation calling the nation to prayer. Then Saunders wrote what he considered an appropriate "Prayer for Peace" and printed it. It was read in most Jackson churches and at the Tomb of the Unknown Soldier on Memorial Day, with radio carrying the program nationwide. Again in 1949 the request for designating Memorial Day as a day of prayer was approved by Congress and the president, and in 1950 a resolution was passed calling on the president to proclaim observation of each Memorial Day by prayer. For his 1949 work, Saunders received the Pulitzer Prize. After the award, requests for his editorial and prayer were so numerous that the *Citizen Patriot* printed a pamphlet containing them to meet the demand. Included here are the 1949 editorial and "Prayer for Peace."

A year ago the *Citizen Patriot* proposed that a period during Memorial day be set aside to pray for peace.

Our suggestion was approved by the Congress of the United States in the form of a resolution sponsored by Senator Homer Ferguson and

Representative Earl C. Michener. The resolution called upon President Truman to proclaim a period of Memorial day for prayers for peace.

The White House issued the proclamation. From Arlington Cemetery the chief of chaplains of the United States Army delivered the Prayer for Peace, the phrasing of which we proposed.

America, commemorating the memories of the men who have fallen on far scattered battlefields that this nation and its way of life might endure, prayed that further sacrifices of war be avoided.

What's more logical than that Memorial day be marked by such a Prayer for Peace?

We recite these circumstances only for the purpose of urging that again this year the President proclaim a period of Memorial day as the proper occasion for nation-wide supplication for peace.

Last year the original suggestion was made only two weeks before Memorial day. This year we make the suggestion early enough to permit normal, routine procedure in Congress and again we remind our readers that this is inspired only with realization that armaments and men alone cannot mold the shape of things to come in this world. First things should come first, and a nation which believes in God should not depend upon the materialism of earth to save it from the great tragedy of war.

We repeat in part the editorial of last May:

"The United States is generally classified as a 'Christian nation.'

"If this means anything at all, it means that the vast majority of our people accept the basic tenets of Christian faith. Beyond that there is a large minority of Americans who worship in the Hebrew faith. Both Christian and Hebrew believe in God as the maker of Heaven and earth.

"Yet as a nation we seem utterly unaware of God or His place in the making of history."

As individuals many Americans worship. Many pray to God daily or more often.

Why then should not America pray as a nation in the time when as a nation we are in dire need of help and guidance?

We do have one day in the year supposedly dedicated to Thanksgiving when we as a people are expected to offer thanks to the Supreme Being for the blessings showered upon us.

But we have no day or hour or minute when as a people we turn to prayer.

If we are a Christian nation, isn't a national moment of prayer a logical, natural course?

Differences in creeds or systems of worship or dogma need not enter into this discussion if as a people we believe that there is a God who shapes the course of our lives.

It should be possible for Protestants, Catholics, Jews and others to join in a common appeal to a common God.

The world is troubled today. America is deeply troubled. The threat of war hangs over all of us. Yet we want peace. We are not a warlike people. We cherish the lives of those young people who become sacrifices in war. We are ready to be tolerant of all nations which do not menace us regardless of divergent ideologies.

So far as this newspaper is concerned, it believes that the preparation for defense of our country is wise and is not in contravention of basic religious beliefs. We appreciate, of course, that some good people disagree with us. They do not believe a fire department is needed to protect us from war's flames even though conflagration threatens.

But first things should come first.

And the first defense against disaster should be prayer. The first appeal for peace should be to the Omnipotent Master of the universe.

Prayer for Peace

O Lord, Father of All Men, We come to Thee in humble supplication.

Thou knowest we have strayed much from Thy laws.

Yet, O God, Thou hast blessed us abundantly, and our children.

Thankful for these blessings and hopeful in the promise of Thy forgiveness, we now beseech Thy special guidance and care.

Again in this world of mortal men wars and threats of wars beset us.

Jealousies and rivalries of nations plague us.

Fears are all about us.

We turn to Thee, O God, to ask that in Thy good time peace may be restored to all nations of men.

We ask that men may live together in understanding and respect.

We ask that governments may rule in Thy wisdom.

We ask that intolerance, bigotry, and greed as between nations, and men, and races, may be overcome by the force of Thy will.

We ask that this United States and its people may be guided by Thee and that its mothers may be spared the sorrows and its sons the sacrifices of further wars.

Bless our leaders with wisdom.

Show us the way to better understanding one with another among our own people.

To that end we seek Thy benediction and light, ready always in faith that Thy will be done and confident that in the end Thy good purpose will triumph. Amen.

Government by Treaty: What We Can Do About It

(DECEMBER 18, 1950)

(for a series on "government by treaty")

WILLIAM H. FITZPATRICK
New Orleans States

WITH the United Nations' adoption of the Universal Declaration of Human Rights in 1948, the United Nations began construction of a "Covenant on Human Rights." Supporters termed it an international bill of civil rights, guaranteeing the basic rights fundamental to the Western system of justice. Some Americans, though, saw the proposed Covenant as a danger to their traditional rights. The Covenant with its conditional guarantees of freedom, they felt, would allow unacceptable restrictions to be placed on the exercise of these rights. In two series of articles in December of 1950, William H. Fitzpatrick, editor of the *New Orleans States,* set forth what he saw as the dangers the Covenant posed to the United States Constitution. The four editorials in a series entitled "The Covenant on Human Rights" discussed the dangers to constitutional rights. A second series, "Government by Treaty," analyzed how a treaty adopting the Covenant would supercede constitutional law. In 1953, reacting to sentiment against adoption of the Covenant and to a movement to amend the Constitution to limit the authority of treaties, the Eisenhower administration announced it would not submit any human rights agreements to the Senate for ratification. This ended any chance the Covenant might have had for U.S. approval. Included here is the final editorial in Fitzpatrick's three-part series on "Government by Treaty."

THIS newspaper is opposed to government by treaty. This newspaper is opposed to ratification of the Genocide Convention and the Covenant on Human Rights, because it believes them to be dangerous to our liberties and freedoms.

Members of the American Bar Association's Committee on Peace and Law through the United Nations ask:

"Can we sacrifice fundamental principles of freedom on the altar of necessity for a compromise?

"For which standard of free speech and a free press will we be fighting under the banner of the United Nations—the standard of the Covenant or the standard of the Constitution of the United States?"

Proponents of these treaties say that we must ratify them to assume the leadership expected of this nation in the conflict of ideologies and the battle for men's minds.

But is it leadership to endanger the rights of our citizens to meet upon the common ground of agreement with other countries whose nationals do not possess nor understand nor, in some cases, desire the rights we as Americans hold dear?

If the government's policy is to set an example, then we recommend the example set by the representatives of the United States, Great Britain and Canada in refusing to approve the proposed Treaty on Public Information because it included the same sort of general restrictions of public safety and public security that the Covenant includes.

But if the policy of our government is to agree to these lower standards on the premise that forsaking our own historic ideals is necessary in the interest of world peace and understanding, then there is a way to implement that policy of compromise and still maintain our own traditional rights and freedoms.

This can be done by amending the Constitution to:

Forbid the invasion of domestic law by treaty unless specifically authorized by Act of Congress;

Forbid the Congress to make treaties effective by laws not otherwise authorized by the Constitution; and

Forbid any fundamental change in our form of government as now constituted by the device of treaty ratification.

The American Bar Association has authorized a committee to study this suggestion of amending the Constitution to protect our Bill of Rights. But until these three steps—or some equally acceptable safeguards—are adopted to prevent destruction of the United States Constitution through government by treaty, the Senate should reject summarily any and all treaties which are judged to contain unacceptable restrictions on and derogations of our rights as free Americans.

The Low Estate of Public Morals

(AUGUST 6, 1951)

LOUIS LaCOSS

St. Louis Globe-Democrat

"THE LOW ESTATE OF PUBLIC MORALS" may have evoked more public response than any other Pulitzer Prize editorial. Numerous letters and telegrams to the *St. Louis Globe-Democrat* applauded Louis LaCoss's stand, and around 50,000 requests were received for reprints. The editorial was inspired by a cheating scandal at the West Point Military Academy, but LaCoss tied the scandal into the climate of dishonesty and low morals throughout America. "The editorial," LaCoss surmised, "said nothing particularly new—I had written many times previously on the general subject—but, as reader response indicated, it packaged the thinking of many Americans." Following publication of the editorial, the *Globe-Democrat* received a volume of suggestions from readers that resulted in a series of articles by leading Americans on solutions to the problem of public immorality. Now, more than a quarter-century after the editorial, an era marked by scandal in government, in public life—an era in which we perhaps have come to accept cheating among our officials, our students, our university sports programs—it may be difficult to comprehend how LaCoss's editorial could have elicited so strong a public response. In 1976 another cheating scandal shook the Army academy. Two years later, 86 of the cadets involved in the scandal were graduated.

THE discharge of 90 West Point cadets for cheating at examinations is only one facet of the many-sided problem of moral disintegration nationally that is causing many persons to wonder whether America is going down the path of decay that caused the Roman empire to fall. It is a sobering thought. But the facts must be faced.

The West Pointers were dishonest. They cheated. Some did so because they couldn't play football and keep up with their studies. Others who were not athletes cheated because that was the easy way to make passing grades.

The excuse of the athletes accents the abnormality of thinking in many institutions of higher education as to the part sports should play in college life. The necessity of having a good team to assure big revenue to build a bigger stadium to make more money, has led many of our colleges into the evil devices of buying players, of competing in the open market for a star half back. Some colleges have recognized the error and have de-emphasized sports, as should be done.

At West Point the incentive was a bit different because Uncle Sam foots the bills there, but there was the incentive for the individual to "make" the team that was tops or near it in the nation. So, if practice on the field interfered, cheat a little and make the necessary grades.

But fundamentally what happened at West Point reflects a present distorted attitude toward old-fashioned honesty and integrity that obtains not only in our schools but in America's social and political life.

It is seen in the high places in government, which after World War II practiced plain deception on the people. We were told no secret agreements had been made with anybody. Later, we discovered pacts were signed at Tehran, Yalta and Potsdam that made the Korean war inevitable.

In the New Deal era was born the idea that an administration can perpetuate itself in power by buying the voters with handout money. Remember how Harry Hopkins tapped the WPA till to win an election in Kentucky? During that era was born the fiction that cities and states as well as individuals need not look to their own resources or ingenuity to survive—let Washington do it. Out of the mating of depression and political trickery came the insidious thinking by millions of Americans that hard work is positively silly; that if one does work, do the least possible, draw the biggest pay possible—and strike for more.

The youths, such as the West Pointers, with whom we are concerned today, were babies then. They have grown into manhood in an environment of take-it-where-I-find-it entirely alien to the American tradition. They are the unpretty fruit of the mistakes of the past two decades.

What do we see in Washington today? Corruption and scandals. The close link between the underworld and politics was revealed by the Kefauver committee. The Fulbright committee turned the spotlight on the RFC and the influence peddlers, some within the shadow of the White House, who sold their contacts for a price.

We hear of doubtful goings-on in the government department that collects our income taxes.

We hear of patronage bought and sold like so much goods over the counter.

An Army General sees no wrong in accepting gifts from those with whom he does government business, nor in diverting government materials to private use.

The chairman of the Democratic National Committee yells "smear" when it is discovered that he is on the pay roll of a St. Louis company for the ostensible reason that he has influence on RFC loans.

The close personal friend of the President, a Major General, has a desk in the White House where he conveniently hands out receipts for deep freezers presented him gratis and which he distributes where they will do good politically.

Campaigns for the Senate in Ohio and Maryland last year were conducted along lines that set a new political low.

So, when 90 West Point cadets stray from paths of honesty, when nauseous revelations are made of the bribing of college basketball teams, when youths charged with robbery stand up in court, as they did in New York, and brazenly admit their guilt, but excuse it by saying that "everybody's doing it," when teenagers become delinquent via the narcotics road, when too many youths of both sexes flout the laws of chastity and decency—when these derelictions of the youths of our land are totted up, there comes a time for sober questioning among the adults.

Where does the fault lie? In the home? Perhaps. In the schools? In part. In the churches? In part. But in the main the fault lies in that nebulous field of public morals and spirituality which was so highly cultivated by the founding fathers and which of late has been so scantily tilled. Among too many of us the accepted premise is that anything is fair unless we are caught; that each of us is entitled to something for nothing; that the world owes us a living; that an honest day's work for an honest day's pay is almost unethical; that gypping the other fellow before he gyps you is the only policy that pays off.

The level of public morals is low. Unfortunately, the good example is not set in Washington. The President is victimized by his friends, but a false sense of loyalty prevents him from moving forthright against them. His reluctance condones wrong-doing. Leadership in both parties is weak, because it is consistently attuned to the next election, not to what is best for the public welfare. In fact, public morals are low because politics at all levels is played at an historic low. The one is the coadjutor of the other.

Yet, we strut the earth telling everybody else to look at us and see democracy in fairest flower—and please copy; we'll foot the bill. We wonder, for instance, what Pravda will have to say about the 90 West Point cadets.

The time is here for moral regeneration. West Point is just one item in the sad chronology. The Roman empire fell, not because it was overwhelmed from without, but because it decayed from within. If this is an appeal for a return to the day-by-day practice of old time religion, and respect for God's moral law, so be it. When the moral fabric of a nation begins to unravel, it is time to do some patching before the entire garment is gone. The cause and effect of this deterioration nationally will be issues in next year's presidential campaign.

The Quality of Morality

(NOVEMBER 12, 1952)

(for distinguished editorial writing)

VERMONT CONNECTICUT ROYSTER
Wall Street Journal

"THE QUALITY OF MORALITY" reminds one of Louis LaCoss's 1952 editorial on public morals. Vermont Connecticut Royster's entry consisted of 13 editorials covering topics from politics to Christianity and from prizefighting to public morality. The Pulitzer Advisory Board cited Royster for his "ability to decide the underlying and moral issue, illuminated by a deep faith and confidence in people of our country . . . [and his] warmth, simplicity and understanding of the basic outlooks of American people." It mentioned the editorial included here as typical of his work. Written shortly after the 1952 presidential election, the editorial attempts to analyze Eisenhower's defeat of Adlai Stevenson as a difference between their stands on moral issues. While the editorial is commendable for its effort at perceiving underlying principles, there is a question of whether Royster adequately defines "morality" in equating it with such issues as inflation. His definition also includes a strong correspondence of morality to Republicanism, and the question immediately arises of whether Democrats would have argued that their social policies showed more concern for humanity than Republican policies did and, thus, deeper morality.

ONE of the puzzlements of the politicians and political commentators over the election seems to be that the people voted overwhelmingly against the Administration during a period when the country is supposed to be prosperous.

Well, the first question raised by the election is whether the people thought themselves as "prosperous" as they were told they were. What was exploded as a myth may have been all this talk about good times for everybody.

It is true enough that an inflation seems to make a lot of people better off than otherwise. But a lot of other people are obviously worse off. And still more people who at first think they are better off soon find that they are not, even though they may be told over and over that they are.

The simple fact is that inflation does not make good times. It makes bad times. Long continued, it makes the worst of times. The election figures suggest that a great many people have discovered that fact.

And to us the election figures suggest one other fact—or at least one other quality in the American people deeply imbedded in their history. That is the quality which when the crucial moment comes makes a moral issue ascendant above all others.

In 1862 someone asked Lincoln where he differed with Mr. Douglas, since both would preserve the union, both opposed the extension of slavery, both would leave it alone where it was. Mr. Lincoln said only on a moral issue: he believed slavery was wrong, Mr. Douglas believed it was all right, and that in the end the moral answer would override all else. A century's veneration is tribute to Lincoln's understanding of his fellow citizens.

In 1952 the electorate was presented with a moral issue. Often on specific programs it was difficult to tell Mr. Eisenhower from Mr. Stevenson; Republican policies from Democratic ones. But there was a great difference in the answer to one simple question.

Was the sort of government we were getting right or wrong?

Mr. Stevenson perforce said it was right. Mr. Stevenson agreed that corruption and betrayal and inflation and all the rest were bad. But perforce he argued extenuating circumstances. He could not be morally indignant about our government without disowning his own party and its erstwhile leader.

Mr. Eisenhower said the kind of government we have been getting was wrong. He said inflation was wrong not only because it was bad economics but because it robbed people. He said the present Korean situation was wrong because there was in sight no end to the slaughter. He said big and omnipotent government was wrong not merely because it was unmanageable but because it deprived people of their liberties.

Mr. Eisenhower won the people, we think, because he said corruption, Communism, inflation, war waste and all the rest were morally wrong. He appealed not to cupidity but to the sense of right and wrong.

In an adjacent column Mr. Chamberlin reminds us of great nations that fell because the people could be debauched to the point where they were no longer capable of moral indignation.

We do not think Americans are immune to human frailties. Other things being equal they can be grateful for bread and circuses and express their gratitude at the polls. But present them a moral issue and nothing else is equal.

Once convince the people of a moral issue, be it at city hall or Capitol Hill, and they will set aside even cupidity. Long is the list—and now longer—of the would-be buyers of the electorate who have had their power snatched from them by the people's moral indignation.

Still Wanted: A New Look—1
(DECEMBER 2, 1953)

(for a series on the "new look" in national defense)

DON MURRAY
Boston Herald

DON MURRAY'S entry of more than 100 editorials was the largest ever submitted for the Pulitzer Prize. Yet all the editorials were part of a series on a proposed "new look" in national defense. To gather information for the series, Murray interviewed experts in Congress and the military, made field studies and examined numerous documents. His goal in the series was to analyze changes in U.S. military policy and examine means of improving America's defense capabilities. The editorials were critical but constructive and were creditable enough to be cited in congressional debates. Reprinted below is the first article of the series. From it, Murray's outlook and approach should be clear. He strongly favors military power but does not agree blindly with military practice in developing a defense program. Instead, he analytically examines the question of why American defense was muddled and calls for a well-defined policy arrived at free of military bureaucracy. Murray, at age 29, was the youngest editorial writer to ever receive the Pulitzer.

IT is eight years since the United States stood victor in two wars—one in the Pacific and one in Europe.

It is four years since Russia exploded our monopoly of atomic weapons. It is three-and-a-half years since Communist forces invaded South Korea.

Yet we still do not have a long range military policy, with well defined goals and priorities, which would make steady, efficient military growth possible.

Unprepared for every war in our history, we run a great danger of being unprepared for another. For while we have spent huge sums for defense there is evidence we have not spent it all effectively. We have allocated our dollars in wasteful fits and starts, instead of by orderly plan.

The absence of a military policy motivates this series of editorials. We will show:

(1) Why we don't have a long term military policy.

(2) Why one is essential now.

We will suggest:

(1) What our military policy should include.

(2) How it can be created.

This is why we don't have a military policy today.

The new Joint Chiefs of Staff sat down in chains to formulate a fresh military policy.

The Secretary of Defense had indicated their budget was not to exceed $35,000,000,000, a sharp cut from the interim budget adopted earlier in the year.

The administration was not prepared to eliminate any of the commitments made under larger budgets. We were still to keep troops in Europe and Korea, navies on both oceans, air bases on four continents—all as we probably should.

But our foreign commitments and our fiscal restrictions closed off two main avenues to a new look. In a meeting at Quantico the President indicated he would not tolerate any dissension within the Joint Chiefs of Staff. They turned to themselves. Admiral Radford announced they would meet alone—without advisers—and he brought the Marines in as an equal member whenever possible.

With understandable but dangerous dedication, each head of his service fought for his men. Blinded by years of service devotion, apparently unable to accept the deep meanings of new weapons and new ways to carry them to battle, the Joint Chiefs of Staff ran to an unhappy compromise.

They adopted the interim budget drafted in haste by the new administration last spring. It had, of necessity, been made without thorough investigation or profound military consideration.

But the JCS turned to it, for it maintained the Army and Navy at their present high levels. The Air Force, unable to appeal, accepted their previously established cut, even though it, alone of all the services, is in the middle of a building program. The Air Force may have had little choice. The other services had the votes.

This budget was passed by the Defense Department to the National Security Council. There it was turned down and sent back to the military.

Why? Because the Secretary of the Treasury said it cost too much and because other members of the Council recognized that it was no new look. And the people had been promised a new look.

At the moment a special committee of junior officers, according to *Fortune* magazine, are trying to come up with a new look. We'd like to bet that it's more of a barroom brawl than a profound re-evaluation of our military situation. The men on this committee may justifiably believe that their career depends on what they get for their service, not what they accomplish for the country.

In future editorials we will show how important it is we correct this situation and how we may go about it.

An Instance of Costly Cause and Effect
Which Detroiters Should Weigh Soberly
(JULY 16, 1954)

1955

ROYCE HOWES
Detroit Free Press

THE editorial for which Royce Howes won the 1955 Pulitzer is as much a reporting job as an editorial one. In a work of about 2,000 words, Howes attempts to explain why laborers at a Dodge automotive plant in Detroit went on strike. He was aided by two *Free Press* reporters who helped gather information. Though the editorial is successful as a news report, Howes also attempts to make a point: that the city and its residents could not afford strikes based on "insignificant" causes. The editorial attempts to place the blame for such a strike on both management and labor. Indeed, the Pulitzer jury lauded it for "impartially . . . analyzing the responsibility" of the two groups. But a hint of management favoritism is apparent. Howes, formerly a public relations employee for a Detroit steel company, does not adequately emphasize the significance of the "little holes" that were the point of the strike. It was not the holes themselves (to which Howes gives exaggerated emphasis) but the amount of work expected of laborers that was the crux of the trouble. When this is recognized, Howes's contention that the strike was for a frivolous reason becomes questionable. Thus the central theme of the editorial is opened to challenge.

IN auto shops the strip which frames the insides of your car's windows is called garnish molding. Screws hold it in place, and of course, there must be holes for the screws.

How many of those holes can reasonably be drilled in eight hours by Dodge assembly line men was the seed of the disagreement which last week made almost 45,000 Chrysler Corporation workers idle and payless.

The insignificance of the little hole in contrast to the immensity of loss to all whom the strike touched reminds of nothing so much as the old nursery rhyme that tells how what began with the loss of a horseshoe nail ended with the loss of a kingdom.

The question we want to examine here is whether Detroit can afford that kind of cause-and-effect sequence.

We are not thinking of just the pay which the strike cost Chrysler workers who participated or whose jobs stopped temporarily because of the strike. Nor are we considering primarily the cost to the corporation in production and dislocation. And while we are not forgetting all the merchants of goods and services whose cash registers rang up less money because so many were out of work, that isn't the cause of our primary concern, either.

What troubles us most gravely is the long-term damage to Detroit as a place to prosper, whether you are a production worker, management man or merchant. Accumulatively, affairs such as last week's strike hurt Detroit's reputation. And when its reputation goes, hope of an ever-building prosperity goes with it.

Industries do not like to locate, or even continue, in a place where the trivial can cost so much. Workmen don't like to establish where instability is so great that a triviality can cost them a week's pay—or more.

We would not attempt to allocate the degrees of responsibility for the Chrysler Corporation stoppage last week.

Nor do we contend that either union or management should have shrugged off everything as trivial that occurred between the disagreement over drilling little holes and the idling of nearly 45,000.

After all, between loss of the horseshoe nail and loss of the kingdom events became increasingly less trivial. So with the progress of the dispute at Dodge.

What happened was this, and here we relate the company's story and then the Dodge local's version:

Until June 28, there were 26 men installing garnish moldings. Each accomplished the entire process. The molding was adjusted, clamped in place, holes drilled, screws driven and clamp removed by the individual man.

On that day, following an efficiency study, engineers changed the operation. A man did just one thing in the installation process. Those who fitted didn't clamp, those who clamped didn't drill, and so on.

One thing this did was to enable a man to work more or less in place as the car passed him. Formerly he rode down the line in the car and walked as much as 100 feet back to resume his station. In time, it was anticipated, the new way would reduce the garnish molding crew to 18 men and permit transfer of the other eight to new work.

The system, according to the engineers, has been used for some time in almost all—and perhaps all—other auto plants. They say it involves no speed-up, but a greater production proficiency.

Under this plan at Dodge, four men were assigned the drilling job.

July 12, one of them was warned he was not keeping pace and causing other drillers to lose position. The next day he was sent home, and the three other drillers were warned that they were not keeping up to standard. At the same time, extra drillers were assigned.

July 14, the drillers again lost position, extra ones were added and supervisors demonstrated how the job could be done without losing position. But the next day the other three original drillers lost position so rapidly that they fell 15 cars behind.

They were sent home and warned that they would be discharged if their work wasn't satisfactory when they came back. This brought a resentment among other workers, the line became jammed, it had to be shut down and 5,000 men were sent home.

The next day two of the drillers returned, failed to turn in the work required of them and were fired. That was a Friday. Nearly 100 men didn't return from lunch, the line had to be stopped once more and the next Monday the strike was called—so improperly, it now turns out, that it had no legality in the eyes of not only management but of the UAW.

Officials of the Dodge local say that with the change of procedure in the matter of garnish molding there was no chance for a "rest break" possible formerly because a man could get his immediate job done by working fast and finishing it in less than the required time. Now, the local says the next job is constantly waiting and a 10-minute relief can be had only when the foreman grants it.

No time study, says the union, has been made, though in early July a grievance was filed and such a study requested. The management asked that the study be postponed 30 days to give men opportunity to accustom themselves to the new system. That would be necessary, it was explained, to determine actually what the method should call for in work output.

What has happened, says the local, is that production line manpower is set up to handle an even flow of 75 cars an hour, but frequently must handle 85 cars an hour. This occurs, it is explained, because unavoidable stoppages of the line (breakdowns, absence of materials, etc.) are compensated for by increasing speed so that the day's output averages 75 cars an hour.

The local's version of the discharge of the two men, which touched off the strike, parallels that of the company—except that the company says the firing was "for deliberate refusal to put out a fair day's work and refusing to do what they were told."

First the matter of how and by whom the holes, five in each molding, were to be drilled. Then two men fired. After that close to 45,000 idled.

We don't think very many people will see any necessity for the

drastic consequence of so little. Nor do we think when the cause is analyzed it can do anything but bring harm to the whole city.

We remarked that we would not attempt to assess degrees of
responsibility—not exact degrees.

But it seems apparent that the Dodge local was anything but free of
fault. In fact that much was ruled Friday when the parent UAW ordered
the strike called off and said that the vote under which it was called was
improper.

Under UAW rules a strike vote must be taken on a specific
grievance, and any subsequent strike actually called can only relate to
that grievance. The vote taken several months ago under which the
Dodge local's leadership acted concerned a matter having nothing to do
with how a garnish molding shall be installed.

Perhaps management let dissatisfaction run too far and get out of
hand. It seems to us there could have, for instance, been a tentative time
study. Its results need not have been final, but at least some guidance
might be had from it and the workers who thought there should be one
somewhat mollified.

The UAW, at the international level, might have been better ad-
vised had it stepped in sooner instead of giving the Dodge local so much
time to work its way out of an untenable position.

The weakness and danger in the union position, as we see it, is that
it endeavors to assume management prerogatives in trying to say how a
plant shall run; what production methods shall be employed; how much
patience must be shown employes who cannot or will not do the same job
which has been demonstrated as reasonable elsewhere.

Names need not be named, but anyone casually acquainted with
Detroit's latter day industrial picture knows that just such relin-
quishments of management function have had a prominent part in the
departure from this region of certain industries, and the abolishment of
thousands of jobs forever.

It is the condition which drives industry from a place. It is prominent among the reasons why some industries have not been able to meet
the challenge of competition.

What labor shall receive in wages, what hours it will work, what
benefits it will receive are properly matters for the union in collective
bargaining. So are working conditions free from avoidable hazard to
safety. Other items proper to union bargaining can be named.

But assumption of the right to manage is not one of them, and
assumption of that right is inevitably destructive. It can only lead to fewer
jobs.

Firm retention by management of the right to manage, on the other hand, makes more jobs. The plants where work is steady and employment high are those where management—even at the cost of riding out strikes—has kept a firm grip on its right to say how things shall be done and what standards those who ask employment will be expected to meet.

We believe that realization of this fact of life is extremely essential to meet.

Ours is a tremendous industrial city, its might and prosperity rest on the payrolls of industry in very great part. There is every reason to believe that unless unnecessary discouragements to industrial growth are presented it will attract more industrial wealth, offer more jobs and increased security.

But what is reflected in the strike and compelled shutdown which put almost 45,000 men and women on the street is a definite and emphatic discouragement. Such exhibitions can turn enterprise from Detroit despite a great many factors here which normally would attract it—as they have attracted it in the past.

Our purpose in discussing the incident of the Dodge strike is not to castigate any individuals or groups as such. But we do believe it represents something which Detroit can ill afford. And our interest in this city's welfare requires that we cite to *Free Press* readers the implications and the portents involved.

What they point to is something neither Detroit nor any other community can afford if its people and its institutions want to maintain a competitive position—and we are thinking of men and women who must compete for jobs just as much as we are of industries which compete for markets.

If the Russians Want More Meat . . .

(FEBRUARY 10, 1955)

LAUREN K. SOTH

Des Moines Register and Tribune

RARE are the editorials that have an effect on a major public event. Lauren K. Soth's "If the Russians Want More Meat . . ." is one of those rare editorials. During the midst of the Cold War, he suggested that Russia send a delegation to Iowa to study agricultural methods. The invitation was made casually, and Soth did not believe it had a chance of being accepted. But it was, and it opened up a program of exchanges between Russia and the United States, helping to thaw somewhat the Cold War. A Russian delegation visited Iowa farms and later introduced Iowan methods to their country's agriculture. In return, an American delegation was invited to Russia. Soth, who toured with the group, wrote that Russia remained secretive but "the freedom we had was a far cry from the way foreigners have been treated in Russia during most of the last ten years."

NIKITA KHRUSHCHEV, who seems to be the real boss of the Soviet Union now, signaled his emergence to power by a well-publicized speech before the Central Committee last month, lambasting the performance of the Soviet economic managers. In this speech Khrushchev especially attacked the management of agriculture. And in doing so, he took the rare line of praising the United States.

Khrushchev advocated the development of feed-livestock agriculture as in the United States. "Americans have succeeded in achieving a high level of animal husbandry," he said. He urged Soviet collective and state farms to plant hybrid corn to provide more feed for livestock. And he demanded an eightfold increase in corn production by 1960.

Speaking as an Iowan, living in the heart of the greatest feed-livestock area of the world, we wish to say that, for once, the Soviet leader is talking sense. That's just what the Russian economy needs—more and better livestock so the Russian people can eat better.

We have no diplomatic authority of any kind, but we hereby extend an invitation to any delegation Khrushchev wants to select to come to

Iowa to get the lowdown on raising high quality cattle, hogs, sheep, and chickens. We promise to hide none of our "secrets." We will take the visiting delegation to Iowa's great agricultural experiment station at Ames, to some of the leading farmers of Iowa, to our livestock breeders, soil conservation experts, and seed companies. Let the Russians see how we do it.

Furthermore, we would be glad to go to Russia with a delegation of Iowa farmers, agronomists, livestock specialists, and other technical authorities. Everything we Iowans know about corn, other feed grains, forage crops, meat animals, and the dairy and poultry industries will be available to the Russians for the asking.

We ask nothing in return. We figure that more knowledge about the means to a good life in Russia can only benefit the world and us. It might even shake the Soviet leaders in their conviction that the United States wants war; it might even persuade them that there is a happier future in developing a high level of living than in this paralyzing race for more and more armaments.

Of course the Russians wouldn't do it. And we doubt even that our own government would dare to permit an adventure in human understanding of this sort. But it *would* make sense.

What a Price for Peace

(FEBRUARY 7, 1956)

(for a series on the issue of segregation)

BUFORD   BOONE

Tuscaloosa (Ala.) *News*

AUTHERINE LUCY was the first black person to enroll at the University of Alabama. There was harsh opposition from the beginning. Admission was granted under order of the U.S. Supreme Court, but even then university officials refused to give her a room or cafeteria privileges. On the nights after Miss Lucy's first two days of class—Friday, February 3, 1956, and Saturday, February 4—crowds gathered on campus. Students made up a large portion of the crowds, but their numbers were swelled by townspeople, high school students, and nonlocal members of extreme prosegregation groups. By noon Monday, a crowd of some 1,000 students and outsiders had grown unruly, even threatening to lynch the young woman. Finally, she escaped from campus lying on the floor of a highway patrol car that drove through the crowd. That night, the university's board of trustees voted to exclude Miss Lucy "lest greater violence should follow." She subsequently charged that school authorities had conspired to create mob action. In early March the trustees permanently expelled her for her "baseless accusations." Throughout these events, Buford Boone, editor of the local *Tuscaloosa News,* stood up for Miss Lucy's right to be admitted to the university and rebuked his fellow townspeople for their actions, despite the possibility of endangering his paper's circulation and advertising. Eventually, his courage, moderation, and perseverance were credited with giving leadership to his troubled community and allaying some of its opposition to integration. "What a Price for Peace" appeared the day after the trustees' night session barring Miss Lucy.

WHEN mobs start imposing their frenzied will on universities, we have a bad situation.

But that is what has happened at the University of Alabama. And it is a development over which the University of Alabama, the people of this state, and the community of Tuscaloosa should be deeply ashamed—and more than a little afraid.

Our government's authority springs from the will of the people. But their wishes, if we are to be guided by democratic processes, must be expressed by ballot at the polls, by action in the legislative halls, and finally by interpretation from the bench. No intelligent expression ever has come from a crazed mob, and it never will.

And make no mistake. There was a mob, in the worst sense, at the University of Alabama yesterday.

Every person who witnessed the events there with comparative detachment speaks of the tragic nearness with which our great university came to being associated with murder—yes, we said murder.

"If they could have gotten their hands on her, they would have killed her."

That was the considered judgment, often expressed, of the many who watched the action without participating in it.

The target was Autherine Lucy. Her "crimes"? She was born black, and she was moving against Southern custom and tradition—but with the law, right on up to the United States Supreme Court, on her side.

What does it mean today at the University of Alabama, and here in Tuscaloosa, to have the law on your side?

The answer has to be: Nothing—that is, if a mob disagrees with you and the courts.

As matters now stand, the university administration and trustees have knuckled under to the pressures and desires of the mob. What is to keep the same mob, if uncontrolled again, from taking over in any other field where it decides to impose its wishes? Apparently, nothing.

What is the answer to a mob? We think that is clear. It lies in firm, decisive action. It lies in the use of whatever force is necessary to restrain and subdue anyone who is violating the law.

Not a single university student has been arrested on the campus and that is no indictment against the men in uniform, but against higher levels which failed to give them clean-cut authority to go along with responsibility.

What has happened here is far more important than whether a Negro girl is admitted to the university. We have a breakdown of law and order, an abject surrender to what is expedient rather than a courageous stand for what is right.

Yes, there's peace on the university campus this morning. But what a price has been paid for it!

Reflections in a Hurricane's Eye

(SEPTEMBER 9, 1957)

(for a series on the Little Rock integration conflict)

HARRY S. ASHMORE
Arkansas Gazette

ALMOST a century had passed since a state had defied the federal government with troops, but in 1957 Governor Orval Faubus of Arkansas chose to do so. When nine black students attempted to enroll in Little Rock's Central High School under a federal court decision, the governor chose not to accede but opted for a show of force. On September 2 he called out armed troops of the Arkansas National Guard to bar the students from entering. The *Arkansas Gazette,* one of the city's two daily papers, challenged the governor and the strong prosegregation element of its city. Finally, on September 23, President Dwight Eisenhower moved federal troops into Little Rock to ensure the enrollment of the black students and maintain order. The *Gazette*'s executive editor, Harry Ashmore, said he was never prosegregation and saw the issue as one of the supremacy of the Constitution in all matters. Supported by the paper's 84-year-old editor and president, J. N. Heiskell, Ashmore unswervingly opposed the governor's actions and supported obedience to the law despite threats to the *Gazette*'s circulation and advertising. At one point, circulation fell 11,000, about 10 percent of its total. Anonymous letters, believed inspired by White Citizens Councils, threatened a "massive crusade" against stores advertising in the *Gazette.* The boycott of advertising and circulation cut total revenue by $2 million. Eventually, Ashmore vacated his position to alleviate some of the pressure on the paper. For the "forcefulness, dispassionate analysis and clarity of his editorials" during the integration crisis, he received the Pulitzer Prize. Below is the editorial, with its challenge to Arkansans to "decide what kind of people we are," most widely quoted from Ashmore's writings during that tense autumn.

THIS is written in a moment of relative calm—something like the eye of the hurricane of emotion that has beset this city and this state for the past week and is due to resume in full force a few hours from now when Governor Faubus appears before a national television audience to explain his position and defend it if he can.

Sunday is a good day for calm reflection, and we hope Arkansans are so using it. Sunday is a good day, too, to be reminded that in the current crisis there are questions not only of law and of politics, but of morality.

Somehow, some time the present impasse between Mr. Faubus and the federal courts must be resolved. That is the problem, and it is an extraordinarily complex one, that faces the responsible leaders of the city, the state and the nation. We can assume that they are working on it, and we can pray that they will find a way out before the final show-down of force against force which Mr. Faubus has so far invited.

But it is also an inescapable problem for each one of us. Somehow, some time, every Arkansan is going to have to be counted. We are going to have to decide what kind of people we are—whether we obey the law only when we approve of it, or whether we obey it no matter how distasteful we may find it.

And this, finally, is the only issue before the people of Arkansas. It is quite true that most of us would have preferred to continue segregation in the public schools. But it is equally true that we cannot do so lawfully except with the voluntary consent of the Negro people whose children have been declared legally eligible for admission to schools heretofore reserved for whites.

It is important to remember that for the most part the Negroes of this community have volunteered not to exercise the new privilege guaranteed to them by federal law. They have accepted a plan of integration that involves only a tiny handful of members of their race. They have done so reluctantly on their side, but with good will—because they have recognized that the School Board of Little Rock was proceeding in good faith to work out the best practical solution to what all parties agree is a problem that cries out for time and patience.

This is the spirit in which the great majority of the white and colored people of this community accepted the School Board plan. Only a small and militant minority of whites urged upon Mr. Faubus the extreme course of interposing his state authority directly against the order of a United States Court.

We believe the great majority of whites supported the School Board last Tuesday—and still do despite the sensational events of recent days.

There are those, of course, who admire Mr. Faubus's courage, and in the calculated confusion of the hour have even come to believe that he may yet stand against the government of the United States.

There were also those, we suppose, who admired King Canute when he ordered the sea to turn back. But the sea did not turn back—and there is no indication that the federal government can or will abandon the authority of the United States Supreme Court.

The legal precedent is firm and clear. In the 1930's the governor of Texas called out the National Guard to prevent the enforcement of a federal law. The unanimous opinion written by Chief Justice Hughes concluded:

> If this extreme position could be deemed to be well taken, it is manifest that the fiat of a state Governor, and not the Constitution of the United States, would be the supreme law of the land; that the restrictions of the Federal Constitution upon the exercise of state power would be but impotent phrases, the futility of which the state may at any time disclose by the simple process of transferring powers of legislation to the Governor to be exercised by him, beyond control, upon his assertion of necessity. Under our system of government, such a conclusion is obviously untenable. There is no such avenue of escape from the paramount authority of the Federal Constitution.

This then is the law as interpreted by the Court whose voice on constitutional matters is final. It is the law that in the end will prevail—and on Sunday there must have been many who prayed that its enforcement will not increase the already heavy damage that has been done to the spirit of good will and brotherly love that prevailed before armed, uniformed men suddenly appeared unannounced on our quiet streets.

A Church, A School—

(OCTOBER 15, 1958)

(for distinguished editorial writing)

RALPH McGILL
Atlanta Constitution

RALPH McGILL, editor of the *Atlanta Constitution,* spoke out against the bigotry and prejudice in his region of the nation with a boldness few other southern editors chose or dared to copy. One of his first acts when he became executive editor of the *Constitution* in 1938 was to require that the word "Negro" be spelled with a capital "N." It was a small gesture, but it made the paper perhaps the first in the South to adopt the practice. It also indicated something of McGill's attitudes. Throughout his career he opposed the Ku Klux Klan, bigoted politicians, and any others who used race to foment hatred. On a Sunday afternoon in October 1958 McGill returned home from a speaking trip in Georgia. His wife met him at the door to tell him the Temple, Atlanta's largest Jewish synagogue, had been bombed. McGill, usually a gentle man except when confronting inhumanity, was furious. He went to his office and in 20 minutes of writing produced an editorial of indignation. He headed it "A Church, A School—" and it appeared on the *Constitution*'s front page the next day. This and other editorials about the bombing display McGill's style, sometimes angry, sometimes compassionate, sometimes poignant, humorous, lucid. For these editorials on the bombing, he was awarded the 1959 Pulitzer.

DYNAMITE in great quantity Sunday ripped a beautiful Temple of worship in Atlanta. It followed hard on the heels of a like destruction of a handsome high school at Clinton, Tennessee.

The same rabid, mad-dog minds were, without question, behind both. They also are the source of previous bombings in Florida, Alabama and South Carolina. The school house and the church are the targets of diseased, hate-filled minds.

Let us face the facts.

This is a harvest. It is the crop of things sown.

It is the harvest of defiance of courts and the encouragement of citizens to defy law on the parts of many Southern politicians. It will be grimly humorous if certain state attorneys general issue statements of regret. And it will be quite a job for some editors, columnists and commentators, who have been saying that our courts have no jurisdiction and that the people should refuse to accept their authority, now to deplore.

It is not possible to preach lawlessness and restrict it.

To be sure, none said go bomb a Jewish temple or a school.

But let it be understood that when leadership in high places in any degree fails to support constituted authority, it opens the gates to all those who wish to take law into their hands.

There will be, to be sure, the customary act of the careful drawing aside of skirts on the part of those in high places.

"How awful," they will exclaim. "How terrible. Something must be done."

But the record stands. The extremists of the citizens' councils, the political leaders who in terms violent and inflammatory have repudiated their oaths and stood against due process of law have helped unloose this flood of hate and bombing.

This, too, is a harvest of those so-called Christian ministers who have chosen to preach hate instead of compassion. Let them now find pious words and raise their hands in deploring the bombing of a synagogue.

You do not preach and encourage hatred for the Negro and hope to restrict it to that field. It is an old, old story. It is one repeated over and over again in history. When the wolves of hate are loosed on one people, then no one is safe.

Hate and lawlessness by those who lead release the yellow rats and encourage the crazed and neurotic who print and distribute the hate pamphlets, who shrieked that Franklin Roosevelt was a Jew; who denounce the Supreme Court as being Communist and controlled by Jewish influences.

This series of bombings is the harvest, too, of something else.

One of those connected with the bombing telephoned a news service early Sunday morning to say the job would be done. It was to be committed, he said, by the Confederate Underground.

The Confederacy and the men who led it are revered by millions. Its leaders returned to the Union and urged that the future be committed to building a stronger America. This was particularly true of General Robert E. Lee. Time after time he urged his students at Washington University to forget the War Between the States and to help build a greater and stronger union.

But for too many years now we have seen the Confederate flag and the emotions of that great war become the property of men not fit to tie the shoes of those who fought for it. Some of these have been merely childish and immature. Others have perverted and commercialized the flag by making the Stars and Bars, and the Confederacy itself, a symbol of hate and bombings.

For a long time now it has been needful for all Americans to stand up and be counted on the side of law and the due process of law even when to do so goes against personal beliefs and emotions. It is late. But there is yet time.

The Year Virginia Closed the Schools

(JANUARY 1, 1959)

1 9 6 0

(for a series on school desegregation)

LENOIR CHAMBERS
Norfolk Virginian-Pilot

THE racial difficulties the nation had faced in the 1950s were evident in the first Pulitzer Prize for editorial writing in the sixties. Lenoir Chambers, editor of the *Norfolk Virginian-Pilot,* received the 1960 award for his editorials opposing resistance to integration of schools in his state. (Coincidentally, Chambers had been a journalism student at Columbia University the year the first Pulitzer Prizes were awarded.) Two editorials were cited specifically in the announcement of Chambers's prize. The first, which appears below, criticized state actions in shutting down nine schools in the state to avoid court-ordered integration. In it, Chambers painfully decried the abandonment of the state's educational tradition. The second editorial, entitled "The Year Virginia Opened the Schools," was printed the last day of 1959 and applauded changing attitudes that finally had led to acceptance of integration. Following court decisions in January of that year, public and official reaction at first was defiant, as it had been to earlier orders. But gradually in Norfolk and most other parts of the state the acceptance of integration gained momentum and resistance finally grew scant. "Thus it came about," Chambers wrote on December 31, "that although the first half of the year found Virginia engrossed in immediate, complicated problems, the second half found the state moving calmly about its educational responsibilities."

So far as the future histories of this state can be anticipated now, the year 1958 will be best known as the year Virginia closed the public schools.

This was the year when the automatic operation of Virginia law, moving precisely as the state's governmental leadership and its General Assembly had provided, reached out to shut and lock the doors of a Warren County high school in Front Royal, of two schools in Charlottesville, and of three junior high schools and three high schools in Norfolk.

By that same act the state denied nearly 13,000 boys and girls,

124

some 10,000 of them in Norfolk, the kind of education which the people of Virginia had in mind when they wrote into their Constitution with wide approval and great confidence these words:

"The General Assembly shall establish and *maintain* an efficient system of public free schools *throughout the state.*" (The italics are ours.)

Had anyone said a few years ago that the abandonment of this fundamental doctrine, which generations of Virginians regarded as a foundation of modern life itself, he would have been called foolish and irresponsible [*sic*]. Yet the year 1958 witnessed this blunt reversal of the educational course of democratic America in these three communities in Virginia and for these nearly 13,000 young Virginians.

That is what has made the year just ended unique in Virginia history and, save for another school-closing in Arkansas, unique in American history. That is the shame of 1958.

It is not enough to say, as the state has said in effect, that closing nine schools and kicking nearly 13,000 young people out of public education to shift for themselves is justified by the difficulties of obeying the law.

Of course the difficulties are there. Of course the changing of the customs of decades is painful. Of course perplexities exist and prejudices intrude. Of course law is a hard problem in enforcement and requires the most serious consideration when it runs counter to the deep wishes of majorities of people in a broad region of the country and of Virginia.

No one with knowledge of Southern life thinks there is anything easy about dealing with the situations that confront us all.

But the mark of Virginia's political shame is that in this confusion it found no better method than abandoning public education entirely rather than follow the courts' directions about admitting a few Negro children into all-white schools.

This is not a policy which Virginia can continue. It is so patently self-defeating that calmer judgment would find ways of getting rid of it even if it was not probable as governmental leaders acknowledge that the statutes for closing schools will be declared unconstitutional.

The punishment of innocent children is too severe. The desertion of a doctrine of education on which democracy itself rests runs too much against basic American convictions and beliefs, many of which originated or first found nobility of expression in Virginia. The damage in prestige is too grave. The loss in business, in commerce, in industry in a state which just begins to realize that it has lagged in new efforts in these respects is too costly even in prospect and in early results. It would be disastrous in the long run.

The year that has run out has carried Virginia, and especially Norfolk, where the penalty exacted has been the heaviest, far down a defeatist road. We cannot continue this way. The state is bound by every obligation of governmental principle and human dignity and decency and its own self-interest, to find a better policy than the one we live under.

That policy is collapsing before our eyes. But there will be small gain, or none at all, if in substitution the government of Virginia thinks it can stand still, or move backward in a changing age. It cannot. The question Virginians must ask themselves on this New Year's Day is what they can, and will, do in 1959 to recover from the tragedy of 1958.

The Pastoral Letter

(OCTOBER 22, 1960)

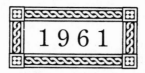

(for editorials on clerical interference in an election)

WILLIAM J. DORVILLIER
San Juan (Puerto Rico) *Star*

WILLIAM DORVILLIER, editor and publisher of the *San Juan Star,* won the 1961 Pulitzer for a series of 20 editorials on clerical influence in the 1960 gubernatorial election in Puerto Rico. He claimed Catholic bishops attempted to interfere in their parishioners' voting, and he called for their transfer by the church. The *Star* received a mountain of letters, protesting and supporting its stand, and kept its columns open fairly to all opinion. Governor Luis Munoz Marin, overwhelmingly re-elected over the opposition of the bishops, wrote Dorvillier after the election: "To adopt such a strong and clear stand on so controversial an issue took great courage. It also set some valuable precedents in Puerto Rican journalism." "The Pastoral Letter" is the first of Dorvillier's editorials. It is indicative of the character and tone of the series.

THE Catholic bishops who signed the pastoral letter forbidding Catholics from voting for the Popular Democratic Party have transgressed grievously against the people of Puerto Rico, against their country and against the Catholic Church.

Archbishop James P. Davis, Bishops James McManus and Luis Aponte Martinex have sinned against the people by making it mandatory that they equate their religious faith with democratic political convictions.

The bishops have sinned against their country by making Puerto Rico the helpless pawn for bigots to use for their political ends, and to injure the Catholic Church in the national campaign.

They have sinned against the Church by making it a temporary synonym for bitterness and hatred, instead of love, among a people who know how to keep their worship and their politics separated.

The bishops have all the rights of citizens to express political opinions and to urge support for their chosen candidates. But they have no right to use their religion and the weight of spiritual sanctions to intimidate faithful Catholics in the exercise of their franchise at the polls.

This pastoral letter is more than an indiscretion. It is an action devoid of any virtue because it so obviously is a result of long and thoughtful premeditation.

Because this pastoral letter is indefensible and inexpiable as an affront to a people who have built a model democracy, we hope Pope John XXIII will transfer the bishops to posts outside Puerto Rico and that they will be replaced by representatives of Catholicism who recognize the indispensability of the principle of separation of church and state in a democracy.

The John Birch Society: An Editorial
(FEBRUARY 26, 1961)

(for editorials on the John Birch Society)

THOMAS M. STORKE
Santa Barbara (Calif.) *News-Press*

THE John Birch Society was formed in 1958. One of the first editors to attack it was Thomas M. Storke, 85-year-old editor and publisher of the *Santa Barbara News-Press*. In explaining his reasons for having his paper challenge the right-wing organization, an editorial stated, "His memory takes him back many years. . . . He lived when conditions were rugged. When West was West and men were men. He lived during periods when if a man or a group of men openly by word of mouth, or the printed word, called our president . . . and others at the head of our government, traitors, they were made to answer. Such slanders often called for a visit from a courageous and irate group which brought with them a barrel of tar and a few feathers. . . . He lived when men were considered cowards when they hid behind their women's skirts and clothed their identity through anonymity." Storke's lead editorial on the Society, which appears below, strikes this theme. The *News-Press* coverage of the Society exposed it to Santa Barbara, and under the paper's leadership the community met the Society with a flood of opposition. Demand for the *News-Press* material about the Society was so great across the nation that the paper issued a special tabloid containing its stories and editorials.

DURING recent weeks, the *News-Press* has sought to enlighten its readers about a semisecret organization called the John Birch Society.

We believe that the *News-Press* has performed a public service by bringing the activities of the society to the attention of the community. Hundreds of our readers have agreed. But a newspaper would be derelict in its duty if it did not express its opinion of the way the society is organized and the tactics it employs.

First, let there be no mistake about this: Communism must be opposed vigorously. Its gains throughout vast areas of the world are shocking. Every American must be alert for Red infiltration. But that does not lead logically to the conclusion that to fight Communism at home we must throw democratic principles and methods into the ashcan and adopt the techniques of the Communists themselves, as the John Birch leaders would have us do.

The *News-Press* condemns the destructive campaign of hate and vilification that the John Birch Society is waging against national leaders who deserve our respect and confidence.

How can anyone follow a leader absurd enough to call former President Eisenhower "a dedicated, conscious agent of the Communist conspiracy"? Those are the words of the national leader of the John Birch Society, Robert Welch, in a manuscript entitled "The Politician," of which photostatic copies are available.

The *News-Press* condemns the dictatorial, undemocratic structure of the society.

The *News-Press* condemns the tactics that have brought anonymous telephone calls of denunciation to Santa Barbarans in recent weeks from members of the John Birch Society or their sympathizers. Among victims of such cowardly diatribes have been educational leaders, including faculty members of the University of California at Santa Barbara, and even ministers of the Gospel.

The *News-Press* condemns the pressures on wealthy residents, who fear and abhor Communism, to contribute money to an organization whose leader has said that "for reasons you will understand, there can be no accounting of funds."

In the Blue Book, the society's "Bible," leader Welch said that the organization needed one million members. He also said that the dues are "whatever the member wants to make them, with a minimum of $24 per year for men and $12 for women."

One million members, divided equally between men and women, would bring him $18 million a year. Quite a sum to play with without accountability!

The *News-Press* challenges members of the society to come into the open and admit membership. A local enrollment "in the hundreds" is claimed, but so far only a few of those who have joined the organization have been unashamed enough to admit it.

The *News-Press* challenges the responsible local leaders of the society to make themselves known.

The *News-Press* challenges them to tell their fellow citizens exactly what they are up to and specifically what program they have in mind for Santa Barbara.

The John Birch Society already has done a grave disservice to Santa Barbara by arousing suspicions and mutual distrust among men of good will. The organization's adherents, sincere in their opposition to

Communism, do not seem to understand the dangers of the totalitarian dynamite with which they are tampering.

The *News-Press* challenges them: Come up from underground.

And if they believe that in being challenged they have grounds for suit—let them sue. The *News-Press* would welcome a suit as a means of shedding more light on the John Birch Society.

Perfectly Capable of Closing Ole Miss

(DATE UNCERTAIN)

(for editorials on an integration crisis in Mississippi)

IRA B. HARKEY, JR.

Pascagoula (Miss.) *Chronicle*

WHEN the courts ordered integration in the South in the 1950s and 1960s, the reaction varied from place to place, but it often involved resistance. In Tuscaloosa, Alabama, mobs threatened a university campus. In Little Rock, Arkansas, the governor called out the National Guard. In most places, though, integration took place with little incident. But in Mississippi, not only did integration result in mob violence and a calling out of federal troops; there was even an attempt to close the state university. At the center of the storm was James Meredith, who broke the color bar and entered the University of Mississippi in 1962. Student mobs grew violent, property was destroyed, death occurred, federal troops moved in to protect Meredith. Ira B. Harkey, Jr., editor of the *Chronicle* in nearby Pascagoula, defied the mob and Mississippi's authorities. For his "courageous editorials devoted to the processes of law and reason" during the crisis, he was awarded the 1963 Pulitzer. Exemplary of his style and argumentation is "Perfectly Capable of Closing Ole Miss," a response to the suggestion that the university be shut down to prevent its integration. But his stand brought him more than a journalism award. The staunch segregationists boycotted his paper, a bullet was fired through his door, and he faced financial ruin. He eventually had to sell the *Chronicle* and move north. In 1966 Meredith was shot while demonstrating for civil rights in Mississippi. The Associated Press photograph of the shooting won a Pulitzer Prize.

ANYWHERE else in the United States, the suggestion that a state university be closed down for any reason at all would not rise to the level of public discussion. Such a suggestion could not originate outside a lunatic academy.

But in our state where the leaders for eight years led us to believe we would not be required to obey the same laws that others must obey, whose leaders called out the mobs to let blood in senseless opposition to the will of the nation, where American GIs and marshals are referred to in terms of hate formerly used only for Huns who ravished Belgium in the World War and Japs who tortured prisoners in World War II—in this state we had better discuss the possibility. Now.

For the people who could do and say the things that have been done and said in our state during the past six weeks have proved themselves perfectly capable of closing down a university.

The suggestion has been made that Ole Miss be closed. It has been offered by the same group of false prophets who deluded the people for eight years into believing that we could maintain school segregation in Mississippi while all about us other Southern states were failing in their attempts to prevent integration. Somehow, in the face of all that is sane, they managed to convince most white people that they had a secret unknown to other Southern leaders.

If we now let them convince us that it is proper to close Ole Miss and destroy a century of cultural advancement, then maybe we do not deserve any better than to be led by owners of grammar-school intellects and of attitudes that most humans left behind somewhere in history.

It is heartening to note a resurgence of manhood on the part of the Ole Miss staff and faculty and the rallying of alumni support to keep the institution going. All alumni, all parents of present students, all Mississippians who care a hang about their state—we will exclude moral and religious considerations here and mention only the economic—all should also rally behind the university and let our leaders know that we do not regard suicide as a solution.

Arrest of Bombing Victim Is Grave Disservice

(MAY 16, 1963)

```
┌─────────────────┐
│      1 9 6 4     │
└─────────────────┘
```

(for steadfast adherence to editorial duty)

HAZEL BRANNON SMITH
Lexington (Miss.) *Advertiser*

WHEN Hazel Brannon Smith received her Pulitzer Prize she was commended for her "steadfast adherence to her editorial duty in the face of great pressure and opposition." The statement was inadequate to describe her real dedication. Mrs. Smith's problems began in 1954 when she criticized a sheriff who shot a young Negro. A local court awarded the sheriff a $10,000 libel verdict. Though the decision was overturned, pressure on Mrs. Smith began to mount. The White Citizens' Council encouraged an advertising boycott of her newspaper. Local residents were induced to drop their subscriptions. A competing paper was begun. After opponents gained control of the local government, Mr. Smith was removed as administrator of the area hospital. The Smiths' financial situation grew critical. They drew from their savings to support their newspaper; they mortgaged their home and built up a debt of $80,000. Still, Mrs. Smith continued her attacks against racists, corrupt local politicians, slot machine operators, gamblers and liquor racketeers. For her stands, she received the 1960 Elijah Lovejoy Award for Courage in Journalism and the 1963 Golden Quill Editorial Award from the International Conference of Weekly Newspaper Editors. When Mrs. Smith was given the 1964 Pulitzer, she described what she saw as her role as an editor: "All we have done here is try to meet honestly the issues as they arose. We did not ask for, nor run from this fight with the White Citizens' Councils. But we have given it all we have, nearly 10 years of our lives, loss of financial security and a big mortgage. We would do the same thing over, if necessary. . . . I could not call myself an editor if I had gone along with the Citizens' Councils—feeling about them the way I do. My interest has been to print the truth and protect and defend the freedom of all Mississippians. It will continue." Included here is the editorial for which Mrs. Smith received the Golden Quill award, one of the editorials in her Pulitzer entry.

It is not moral or just that any man should live in fear, or be compelled to sleep with a loaded gun by his bedside.

HOLMES COUNTY Deputy Sheriff Andrew P. Smith's action in arresting a 58-year-old Negro farmer, Hartman Turnbow, for fire bombing his own home has come as a numbing shock to the people of Holmes County.

It is a grave disservice to our county and all our people in these days of increasing racial tension and strife.

White and Negro citizens of Holmes County alike simply could not believe that something like this could happen in our county, that a man and his wife and 16-year-old daughter could be routed from sleep in the small hours of the morning and be forced to flee their home literally in terror, only to be shot at by intruders outside—then to have the head of the family jailed the same day for doing the dastardly deed by an officer sworn to uphold the law and protect all citizens.

The only evidence presented against the aged Negro man at the preliminary hearing was testimony given by Deputy Smith and that was only an account of the bombing and shooting incident, as reported by Turnbow, to him. Mr. Smith added his own opinions and suppositions, as did County Attorney Pat M. Barrett, who prosecuted the case. As a result the man was bound over under $500 bond for action by the Holmes County Grand Jury in October.

Mr. Barrett, who said he was "not a demolition expert," nevertheless told the Court that "it just couldn't have happened. There is no way on God's earth for that situation over there to have happened like he said it happened."

Four other Negroes, who had been arrested the same day in connection with the same case, were released for lack of evidence. Not one shred of evidence was presented against them. But they had been held in jail five days and five nights.

This kind of conduct on the part of our highest elected peace officer has done serious injury to relations between the races in Holmes County—where we must be able to live in peace and harmony, or not live at all.

It is distressing that no statement has come from Mr. Smith saying that he is continuing his investigation. Perhaps he is. We hope so.

But irreparable damage has been done, and let no one doubt it.

We have always taken pride in being able to manage our affairs ourselves. When we become derelict in our duty and do not faithfully execute our obligations, we may rest assured it will be done for us.

FBI agents and U.S. Justice officials have already made an exhaustive investigation of this bombing and shooting incident.

A suit has already been filed against Deputy Smith, Mr. Barrett and the District Attorney, stating these Negroes were arrested "on false and baseless charges," which were in effect an effort to coerce and intimidate Negro citizens of Holmes County and get them to cease voter registration activity. The Federal suit asks for a permanent injunction to prohibit these officers from interfering with voter registration activities, including the prosecution of the charges now filed against Turnbow, who attempted to register to vote here April 9, and Robert Moses, director of SNCC, a voter registration project.

This kind of situation would never have come about in Holmes County if we had honestly discharged our duties and obligations as citizens in the past; if we had demanded that all citizens be accorded equal treatment and protection under the law. This we have not done.

But if we think the present situation is serious, as indeed, it is, we should take a long, hard look at the future.

It can, and probably will, get infinitely worse—unless we have the necessary character and guts to do something about it—and change the things that need to be changed.

Memo to McKinney

(NOVEMBER 20, 1964)

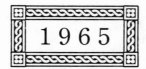

(for editorial campaign for better housing)

JOHN R. HARRISON
Gainesville (Fla.) *Sun*

CIVIC leaders in Gainesville, Florida, had been trying for ten years to get a minimum housing code passed when John R. Harrison began an editorial campaign. Typical of Harrison's writing is "Memo to McKinney," published near the middle of the month-long campaign. The editorial is both descriptive and argumentative. It begins with a scene in one of Gainesville's inadequate housing areas and follows with a criticism of the city's mayor for dragging his feet on housing reform. Whether the quote from Ralph Waldo Emerson in the final paragraph is the most appropriate way to close the editorial can be questioned, but borrowing statements from poets and novelists is not unusual among editorial writers. At the end of Harrison's campaign, Gainesville passed a housing code. When the Pulitzer Prize was awarded, Harrison was commended for serving as a leader for citizens who were helpless by themselves to get the machinery of government to turn for them.

THE road was dusty, and the small Negro boy strained under the weight of the bucket he was carrying. He had brought it more than two blocks from the fountain that was provided "as a courtesy," the sign told us. Three to five times a week the child makes the trip.

The child lives in a house eighteen feet by twenty-four feet along with three other people.

On several of the open windows there are no screens.

There is no front door at all.

Sunlight comes through the roof in two places.

The child and his family share with another family the outhouse in the backyard.

Not only is there no lavatory in the house, there is no tub, shower or hot water supply.

The siding on the house had deteriorated, the chimney needed replacing, the foundation was out of level.

The water lapped over the side of the bucket as the child stepped up a concrete block into the house.

Now, Mayor McKinney, that's a third to a fifth of the family's weekly supply of water.

To drink.

And that family lives in the Northeast section, within the city limits, of Gainesville, Florida, and they pay $5 a week rent. That's Florida's "University City," Center of Science, Education and Medicine.

Now, tell us again, Mayor McKinney, as you have since last August, that a minimum housing code for Gainesville is unnecessary. Tell us again that you want more discussion of the minimum housing code as you did last week. After all, the League of Women Voters and the Citizens' Housing Association of Gainesville, Inc., have, since 1955, documented by studies housing in Gainesville that has no indoor plumbing or piped-in drinking water.

That's ten years, Mr. Mayor.

But tell the child that carries the drinking water down that dusty road that the minimum housing code is unnecessary.

In our mind's eye we'll try to console him with Emerson—"The dice of God are always loaded. For everything you have missed, you have gained something else. The world, turn it how you will, balances it-self. . . . Every secret is told, every virtue rewarded, every wrong re-dressed, in silence and certainty."

The Containment of Ideas
(JANUARY 17, 1965)

(for distinguished editorial writing)

ROBERT LASCH
St. Louis Post-Dispatch

EARLY winners of the Pulitzer Prize were generally pro-American and strongly nationalist. Frank Simonds, Henry Watterson and Frank O'Brien, editorial winners from the World War I era, saw little to criticize in American pro-war policy. In the years of World War II winners such as Ronald Callvert, Bart Howard and Geoffrey Parsons sang praise of the United States and called for unity against its enemies. Editorial winners in the era of the Vietnam War were different. They no longer lauded America. More frequently they criticized. In this vein are the editorials of Robert Lasch. Their general theme is that United States fortunes were poorly served by military involvement in South Vietnam, that force of arms was not the most effective way to combat Communism, that national interests were stronger than ideological interests and would stop the spread of Marxism, and that the best way to contain Communism was to provide a better idea, the idea of freedom. Though the Pulitzer committee stated that the award went to Lasch for the whole of his writing during 1965, it was generally understood that his editorials taking issue with United States foreign policy were highly regarded by the committee. The *Post-Dispatch* specifically noted three editorials it said were cited by the committee. One questioned stated and real American aims in Vietnam. Another asked if the United States were repeating its Cold War mistakes with Russia in its approach to China. The third is reprinted here.

COMING events in South Viet Nam promise for many Americans a profound psychological shock, which a foresighted Administration would be preparing to offset. When the day comes for American forces to leave Viet Nam after 10 years of vain effort to build an anti-Communist bastion there, not only will our national pride be hurt, but some basic assumptions of our postwar foreign policy will be called into question. As fresh think-

139

ing is always more painful than mouthing shibboleths, this is going to cause a certain degree of anguish.

Unpleasant as it may be, the time for reappraisal has come, and thoughtful Americans should resolve to be realistic about it. The first step is to cast off the illusion of omnipotence, under the spell of which many of us have for years assumed that our mission in the world is to contain, roll back, destroy or otherwise combat Communism.

After World War II, the Soviet Union sought to expand its national power wherever possible. The United States, as the leader of the free world, was thoroughly justified in undertaking to contain that thrust, and it was contained. Only where the Red Army stood on land taken from the Nazis—which is to say, only in Eastern Europe—were the Russians able to impose their national will on other peoples; and the passage of time has indicated that even there, subjugation is most likely temporary. National identities have survived and are persistently asserting themselves. There could be no better evidence that the Communists are not going to rule the world, and neither are we. Aspirations for independence, self-respect and self-government are too universal and too powerful to be subdued by any ideology.

In the meantime, however, American policy increasingly has tended to confuse the containment of Russian (and later Chinese) national power with the containment of Communism. We undertook to apply the methods appropriate to a national power struggle—the methods of diplomatic maneuver, armed confrontation and in some cases war itself—in a realm where they are totally ineffective. Communism as an idea cannot be contained by such methods, but only by a better idea.

It is not the American function to combat revolution everywhere—to stand as the universal, all-embracing guardian of the status quo. This is an odd role, by the way, to be thrust upon a nation that was itself born of revolution less than two centuries ago. More important, it is a role that lies beyond the capabilities of any nation. Change is the law of life. Social change will sometimes take revolutionary forms in some countries, no matter what the United States or any other nation thinks about it. A wise foreign policy begins with recognition of this fact.

American foreign policy is in deep trouble in Africa, in Asia, in Latin America precisely because we have let ourselves be pushed into a counter-revolutionary posture. Wherever oppressed masses struggle toward a better life millions of persons look upon the United States as their natural enemy, which means that they inevitably look elsewhere for friends.

Ours is not a revolutionary society, and we should not try to behave as if it were. But we can behave like a mature nation which knows that it has no right and no power to decide for the people of Cuba, Viet Nam or central Africa what form of revolution they should have. We can behave like a nation which is prepared to accept change, even in forms un-palatable to it, and is ready to work with peoples of any political faith for a peaceful world of diversity.

It is often said that we must hang on in Viet Nam, even to the point of an escalated war, because the effects of defeat there would be so damaging elsewhere in Asia and Africa.

Unfortunately it is true that if we got thrown out of Viet Nam, millions of people would be delighted. That is one reason why our Government would be wise to encourage a political settlement through negotiation before we are thrown out unless it is already too late. Whatever happens in Saigon, however, the American cause will not be damaged thereby half so much as it is already being damaged by the growing conviction that our power and influence are dedicated to the sup-pression of social revolution and political change wherever they occur.

We shall improve our position with the developing nations and the world at large not by proving that we can wage endless war in Viet Nam, but by showing, through actual conduct, that the CIA is not enfranchised to swagger around the world setting up governments and knocking them down; that we do not undertake to dictate the form and pace of political change anywhere; that we are prepared to accept revolutions even when we do not approve of them; and that we have enough faith in the ideas of freedom to entrust to them, rather than to arms, the task of containing the ideas of Communism.

Julian Bond Got Used, Too

(JANUARY 12, 1966)

```
┌─────────────────┐
│  1 9 6 7        │
└─────────────────┘
```

(for editorials during the year)

EUGENE PATTERSON
Atlanta Constitution

EUGENE PATTERSON, editor of the *Atlanta Constitution,* was
one of the first to protest the Georgia legislature's attempt to
refuse to seat Julian Bond. The refusal was not because of
Bond's race; a number of Georgia legislators were black. Bond
was a dissident, a critic of United States policy, a foe of the
country's involvement in the Vietnam war and of the Selective
Service law. In the editorial below, Patterson analyzes vividly
the critical moment at which the legislature decided to dis-
qualify Bond. As Patterson predicted in the editorial, Bond's
case was taken to court. Though the legislature's action was
upheld in lower courts, the U.S. Supreme Court held that Bond
was entitled to his seat. At that time, Patterson wrote: "Net
results of this controversy, which the Legislature should never
have initiated, have been to make Julian Bond famous, spread
his views, revive the Student Nonviolent Coordinating Committee and damage Georgia's claim to being a State of wisdom,
justice or moderation. That was a mighty poor return on one
day's blowoff in the Legislature."

THE breaking point in Monday's Bond drama came, it is now plain, when
Speaker George T. Smith asked Julian Bond to rise and answer any con-
cluding questions that members of the Georgia House of Representatives
might wish to ask him. The slight young Negro rose and waited at the
microphone.

He faced no questions. He faced a dead, absolute silence. The
Speaker told him he could sit down.

"I knew right then the House had made up its mind not to seat
him," said a senior observer. "Bond's statements already answered all
the questions there were. The House did not want to touch that fellow—
didn't want anything in the world to do with him. It was all over."

Down the drain went all of the weekend's desperate biracial efforts
to get the young representative seated at least, though censured.

The carefully selected contest committee did meet for a while. Until the day had worn on to the moment of heavy silence, this committee had been expected to recommend seating Bond, while censuring him. Such a recommendation might have passed, too. A large number of representatives were ready to vote for it, on the assumption that the censure motion might have enabled them to survive such a vote back home.

But something was expected of Julian Bond. Some modification, some clarification, some profession of faith in American motives that was not forthcoming as his testimony progressed.

Negro Senator Leroy Johnson and others had labored through the weekend seeking some face-saving formula for him and the House.

A guarded statement from Bond Monday morning seemed to qualify his support slightly for the SNCC statement he had previously endorsed—a statement that amounted to a bitterly cynical indictment not simply of United States policies, but of United States motives and basic honor. But James Foreman or Robert Zellner, the SNCC firebrands, were at Bond's elbow all day. And when he testified in the House chamber Monday afternoon, it was clear he did not mean to temper his position at all. With Bond trapped SNCC could now trap the House (and seems now on the way to trapping Martin Luther King).

The faces of the House slowly froze. Here was a man who was not simply dissenting from U.S. policy, but was accusing his country of murder, deception, aggression; accusing it of being without respect for persons or law; accusing it of using the word freedom as "a hypocritical mask behind which it squashes national liberation movements"; and he was sympathizing with and supporting—even admiring the lawbreaking "courage"—of "men in this country who are unwilling to respond to a military draft."

As the day wore on and Bond hardened in such positions, the House hardened against him. Legal or not, it had decided not to seat him by the time he rose to answer final questions. There were none. Something very close to revulsion lay in the silence.

Bond is an elected representative and a court will probably order his seating, as the House in wisdom should have done. But the record may as well be kept straight. Bond was saying Tuesday that he was attacked because "I am dedicated to the cause of human rights." If that claim were true, it would be a derogation of the nine other Negro legislators and some whites who are also dedicated to the cause of human rights, but are seated with respect in the House and Senate.

Our "Commitments" Open to Question

(MAY 7, 1967)

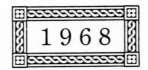

1968

(for distinguished editorial writing)

JOHN S. KNIGHT
Knight Newspapers

ONE of the press's earliest opponents of American involvement in Vietnam was John S. Knight. Born to money, a chain owner who ran his papers as a business, one of the most established of the establishment press publishers, Knight might not have seemed the type to challenge the foreign policy of America. He could not be called unpatriotic, un-American or any of the other epithets thrown at opponents of the U.S. part in the Vietnam war. Though his father, Charles L. Knight, had been a bitter opponent of U.S. participation in World War I, the son volunteered and served with the infantry in the front lines. During World War II he acted as a liaison between America's and Britain's war information offices. Though his oldest son was killed in the war, his youngest still attended a military academy. Besides, at age 72 Knight could not be mistaken for a college student in a protest demonstration. But since 1954, when the French were defeated in Indochina, he had been warning against our presence there. He had been a burr under each presidential administration since. Knight reluctantly entered journalism on his father's paper and began writing editorials in the 1920s. "My father," he said, "to encourage me, told me some of them were good." Since the 1930s he has been writing his "Editor's Notebook," carried weekly in the newspapers in his chain. The column usually is quite long and may cover any of a wide range of topics in Knight's personalized style, which may be light or seriously analytical. His 1968 Pulitzer Prize was awarded for ten of his columns on Vietnam. The one reprinted here demonstrates Knight's analytical, documented, persuasive approach.

THE Senate Republican Policy Committee has issued a thoughtful and presumably well-documented study on the war in Vietnam.

Understandably, it credits the Eisenhower administration with making but a "limited commitment" to the South Vietnamese in 1954 while declaring that "under the Democrats, our commitment has become open ended."

This partisan study faithfully chronicles the mistakes of the Kennedy and Johnson administrations with respect to our involvement in Vietnam. It has caused the *Miami News* to comment that "the seeds of a meaningful dissent have been sown by the Republican party in the Senate."

True perhaps, but where were the dissenting Republicans several years ago when they could have questioned the wisdom of policies they now deplore?

Strangely silent, I submit. Did they fear being tarred as unpatriotic? Or were they coolly calculating that it was politically expedient to support the war while being critical of President Johnson's "mismanagement?"

Whatever the reasons for past GOP strategy, the Republican leadership stands indicted for failing to challenge the successive steps which have brought us to our present dilemma.

Only a handful of courageous Democrats rose in the Senate to pose the searching questions which might better have been advanced by a responsible minority party.

So when the Senate Republican Policy Committee comes now to inquire what our national interests are in Thailand, Cambodia, Vietnam and Laos and to what further lengths "are we prepared to go in support of this interest?" it is proper to ask why the Republicans have delayed so long in seeking this reappraisal.

Is it because their appetites are being whetted by the aroma of "meat a-cookin'" in 1968? Or to wear the mantle of statesmanship even as President Johnson appears to be losing stature?

The Republican Policy Committee, even though Senate minority leader Everett Dirksen looks askance at its report, has made a useful contribution to the debate on Vietnam notwithstanding its partisan approach.

What a pity it is that Senate Republicans did not accept the gauntlet when it was thrown down by the administration years ago.

They must, therefore, bear a goodly share of the responsibility for our growing involvement in Vietnam.

Their inaction—when the times called for courageous dissent—fell far short of the statesmanship to which they now aspire.

How often have we heard politicians intoning that hoary phrase, "we must live up to our commitments," or "the United States always honors its commitments?"

What are our commitments in Vietnam? Who made them? And when and why?

President Johnson says we have a "moral commitment," the same one as "the commitment made by President Eisenhower in 1954."

Secretary of State Dean Rusk assures us that it is a "binding legal commitment" as well.

Actually, three so-called "commitments" are involved. The first was the October 25, 1954, Eisenhower letter to Ngo Dinh Diem, then head of the Saigon government, promising American aid "provided your government is prepared to give assurances as to the standard of performance it would be able to maintain in the event such aid is supplied."

The second "commitment" turned on the SEATO treaty, a collective defense pact signed by the United States, Britain, France, Australia, New Zealand, the Philippines, Pakistan and Thailand.

Our third "commitment" was the Tonkin Gulf resolution as passed by Congress in 1964.

1—As seen in retrospect, the Eisenhower letter was not a commitment but a proposal to give economic aid to South Vietnam if certain conditions for self-help and reform were accepted. Incidentally, these terms were not met.

At no time did President Eisenhower intend to send U.S. military forces to Vietnam, a fact which he readily admits today. And as historian Henry Steele Commager has written, "even had President Eisenhower intended his letter to be a kind of commitment, it would have had no binding force; the President cannot, by private letter, commit the United States to war or quasi-war."

2—The SEATO "commitment" is vague and legalistic, depending upon whether the parties thereto were dealing with "aggression" or "subversion."

The section dealing with aggression provides that whatever measures are taken "shall be immediately reported to the Security Council" of the United Nations.

This step was never taken, although a gesture was made in January of 1966—well after the fact.

The second section under which our "commitment" is defended provides for "collective consultation" in instances of subversion. The late John Foster Dulles, architect of SEATO, so interpreted this provision.

As Senator Walter George of the Foreign Relations Committee said at the time, "the treaty does not call for automatic action, it calls for consultation. All that we are obligated to do is to consult together."

Yet there was no consultation. Although Secretary Rusk talks about "the sanctity of our Pacific alliances," only SEATO members Australia, New Zealand, Thailand and the Philippines have made any contributions to the cause of South Vietnam. France openly opposes U.S. policy, Britain offers only sympathy, Pakistan is disenchanted. So as Commager says, "If our 'honor' is involved, why is not the honor of the other SEATO nations equally involved?"

The American Bar Association upholds our "commitment" in Vietnam on the ground that Article 52 of the United Nations Charter provides for regional agreements for the maintenance of international peace.

It does indeed, but such activities must be "consistent with the purposes and principles of the United Nations" and no enforcement "shall be taken . . . without authorization of the Security Council."

So the question remains: Is the United States committed to unilateral action in Vietnam under the SEATO treaty?

It is my opinion, based upon extensive study of the subject, that we are not committed either legally or morally to our present course of action.

3—The Tonkin Gulf resolution was passed without debate after the North Vietnamese had fired torpedoes at two American destroyers. The resolution pledged support to the President of the United States, as commander-in-chief, to "take all necessary measures to repel any armed attack against the forces of the United States and to prevent further aggression."

The question is now raised as to whether the North Vietnamese committed an act of aggression, since our destroyers were only 11 miles from shore in violation of the "international waters" understanding which is honored by most nations.

When North Vietnam asserted that we had violated her waters, Senator Gaylord Nelson asked on the floor of the Senate: "The patrolling (American destroyers) was for the purpose of demonstrating to the North Vietnamese that we did not recognize a 12-mile limit?" Senator J. W. Fulbright replied: "That was one reason given."

As Mr. Commager has written: "If the Tonkin Gulf affair was a clear case of aggression, why is it that the other members of SEATO have not rallied to our support, as is required by the treaty? If it was a clear case of aggression, why is it that we did not choose to follow the procedure laid down by the charter and submit it to the United Nations?"

Understandably, the American people have little patience with looking backward. One might well say: "Of what value are these facts now? We're in the war, aren't we?"

Yes, we are in the war but we can resent being told on the hour about "our commitments" which at best are but little more than the iterations and reiterations of the President, the Secretary of State and handyman Hubert Humphrey.

As Commager says, "These assertions have in themselves no more authority than had the assertion by the Emperor's tailors that his clothes were indeed regal."

The other argument runs that we have a factual commitment: "We are there whether we like it or not, whether we should be there or not."

Such honored generals as Matthew B. Ridgway, who commanded the UN army in Korea, and James M. Gavin, once Chief of Plans, think we should not be there.

And in the political campaign of 1964, President Lyndon Johnson thought we should not escalate the conflict as is shown by this one quotation from a speech delivered on August 29 of that year:

"I have had advice to load our planes with bombs and to drop them on certain areas that I think would enlarge the war and result in committing a good many American boys to fighting a war that I think ought to be fought by the boys of Asia to protect their own land. And for that reason I haven't chosen to enlarge the war."

When you reread remarks such as this and recall the pretentious predictions of early victory by Defense Secretary McNamara, General Maxwell Taylor and other functionaries, the American people cannot be blamed for their uneasiness over policies which they are unable to understand.

President Johnson does not impress them as a man of candor. He has failed to take them into his confidence, to explain why we are engaged in bloody conflict for objectives which remain obscure and uncertain.

It is not the dissent at home which is prolonging the war.

Rather, it is the determination of the man in the White House—entrapped by pride and circumstances—to bring about a victory or at least an accommodation with honor prior to the 1968 elections.

As history is being written, the possibilities of a wider struggle cannot be discounted.

Nor will our involvement in Vietnam be depicted as one of the glorious eras of American statesmanship.

An Appeal to Reason

(DATE UNCERTAIN)

1969

(for editorials during 1968)

PAUL GREENBERG
Pine Bluff (Ark.) *Commercial*

LIKE the first Pulitzer winner of the 1960s, the last dealt with race relations in the South. Paul Greenberg's editorials from the *Pine Bluff Commercial* that were submitted for the Pulitzer Prize generally were aimed at helping establish better relations between the races locally. Greenberg says his editorials usually attack local problems and even on national issues discuss the local angles. He also attempts to begin with a news peg for his editorial subject and then to "go into the broader issue." In deciding whether to write an editorial, he asks, "Is it worth saying? Does it have originality of message? If the idea is not original, is it worth repeating?" This editorial, written shortly before the 1968 presidential election, is a personalized attempt to persuade local residents not to vote for George Wallace.

WE would like to address today's editorial column especially to those readers who might be considering casting their ballot for president of the United States in favor of George Wallace.

We would like them to consider the reason for the appeal of Mr. Wallace.

Surely it cannot be any experience that George Wallace brings to the great issues of war and peace, and to the awesome responsibilities that await the next president of the United States. Far from claiming any background in foreign affairs, he seldom ventures into the subject. When he does, it is in a primitive fashion. Like threatening to bring France back in line by demanding payment of her war debt, a debt that no longer exists. Most of George Wallace's comments about foreign affairs, infrequent as they are, are no better grounded than this one. We cannot believe that the basis for supporting George Wallace is any widespread demand that the leadership of the United States and of the Western alliance in world affairs be entrusted to the wisdom of George C. Wallace.

It is, then, his stands on the numerous and complex domestic problems of these times? Surely not, since not many people really know where George Wallace stands on farm policy, taxation, the economy, labor, the cities. And not many really much care. Doesn't it say something alarming about George Wallace's appeal that so many people should be attracted on such narrow grounds? Is his one issue enough? It is enough for a talented demagogue, perhaps, but for a president of the United States?

Even when George Wallace talks about law-and-order, which is an issue for sure, the phrase turns cheap in his mouth. Because he is the same George Wallace who has pleaded guilty to contempt of court, who defied the supreme law of the land and threatened order, who only last week predicted a revolution if his demands were not met. Does this sound like a champion of law and order?

It might—if by law and order it meant ignoring the laws one doesn't like and ordering around anybody who gets in one's way. That's the kind of law-and-order that demagogues of both Left and Right always have preached, and preach today.

And there may be times when we are all susceptible to a base appeal. Before that first cup of coffee in the morning, one can almost understand the attraction of George Wallace. Or, if one is black, the attraction of some equal but opposite radical of the Negro race. The most likely explanation for the politics of rancour we are seeing today is that the whole, troubled country is in a bad mood.

Some may find it ironic, or anyway futile, to headline an editorial addressed to Wallace people An Appeal to Reason, since it is not reason but feeling, and often bad feeling at that, that accounts for so much of the Wallace boom. But one of the latest polls shows that something like 20 per cent of the American electorate is attracted to George Wallace; and we can't believe that 1 out of 5 American voters is immune to reason. Or even to second and better thoughts before November 5th is upon us.

Nor can we believe that so many Americans will, for very long, equate George Wallace with the salvation of America. The idea of George Wallace as the man who is going to save the rule of law in America is grotesque; he is not its saviour but a symptom of the defiance that threatens it today.

George Wallace doesn't have a program for the country, only oratory. He says a lot, but what would he do? What could George Wallace do as president against Congress, the courts, the laws already on the books, the rights indelible and still developing in the Constitution, the whole tradition of equal justice before the law?

One of the most revealing, and hopeful, aspects of the Wallace vote is that many of those who plan to cast it don't feel very proud about it. At least not proud enough to argue that George Wallace really ought to be the next president of the United States. Instead, they explain their vote for him as a gesture of protest.

We wonder: Is it right to vote for a man you don't really believe is worthy of the office? Haven't we all been taught that a citizen has a solemn responsibility to cast his vote as if it were the deciding one? Is that principle now outmoded? Is the thrill of protest worth clogging up a venerable and suddenly endangered electoral system? Is this the honorable, the responsible, the patriotic course?

And finally, we wonder if a vote for George Wallace really is a meaningful protest against the unsettling trends that beset this country. Have you noticed how similar the extremes of Left and Right tend to be? George Wallace, for example, keeps talking about those left-wing anarchists who threaten American institutions. But isn't he threatening quite a few himself? Like the Supreme Court and the Electoral College and even the very principle that has been the key to maintaining law and order in this country—that the Constitution and the laws of the United States shall be the supreme law of the land.

Consider that the crucial fight in American politics is not between the extremes of Left and Right. But between the middle—with its sense of proportion and its tolerance of dissent—and both extremes, with their mutual intolerance for the rights of those they dislike. And so maybe the best way to stand up for America, for a nation conceived in liberty and dedicated to the proposition that all men are created equal, for a political system with justice and liberty for all, might be to reject the extremes. And to stick with still another old American institution that George Wallace threatens—the two-party system. Won't you consider it?

Lyndon Johnson's Presidency

(JANUARY 19, 1969)

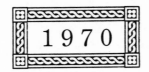

(for editorials during 1969)

PHILIP GEYELIN
Washington Post

ONE of the few Pulitzer winners in the 1970s to deal with non-local issues, Philip Geyelin concentrated on national politics. This seems a natural subject, perhaps even a "local" one, for the editor of the *Washington Post*'s editorial page. In this editorial, as Richard Nixon was about to succeed Lyndon Johnson as president, Geyelin attempts to tell the analytical "story of how Lyndon Johnson lost his majority." The editorial is laudable as an attempt to put contemporary events into historical perspective and as, in places, a lucid analysis. It does tend, however, to jump around from subject to subject with perhaps unnecessary details thrown in, and it seems as if Geyelin simply tries to cover too wide a subject. But such difficulties may just be the usual result when an editorial attempts to analyze an expansive subject in capsule form.

THEY have not been dull, the Johnson years, from the first crisis in Panama to Santo Domingo and South Vietnam, from the wild campaign of 1964 to the triumphs in Congress, the protests on the campus, the riots in the cities and the sudden abdication in 1968. And they have not been unproductive, in their rich yield of civil rights and social welfare legislation. More than anything, perhaps, they have been sad, in the sense that Franklin D. Roosevelt thought of Lincoln as a "sad man because he couldn't get it all at once—and nobody can."

Lyndon Johnson tried, you have to give him that. He brought more raw force and endless energy and craving for accomplishment to the office of President than anyone could ask. Where he succeeded, he succeeded big, in education and civil rights and all the rest. And while it can be said that he also failed big—by not being able to win his way in the war in his time, and by having to acknowledge such a division in the country that he could only carry on in his final year by foreswearing his candidacy for another term—not the least of his legacies to President Nixon is what

152

he himself did to turn the war around and head it in the direction of a gradual American disengagement and a political settlement. Serious peace talking is to begin in Paris this coming week not so much because Lyndon Johnson halted the bombing of North Vietnam in October but because he stared down his generals last March and made the much more difficult decision to refuse them the massive reinforcement of American troops that they were asking for.

If this seems a somewhat negative legacy, there are more than enough that are positive. The list of legislative accomplishments runs on and on from the 1964 Civil Rights Act to rent supplements, voting rights, model cities, medicare, control of water pollution, immigration reform, job training, educational aid. And while some of this was the finishing of unfinished business, well begun before his time, some of it broke new ground. A landmark aid to education act, for elementary and secondary schools, cracked a constitutional and political impasse over church-school relationships, and it was brought into being not by past momentum or by parliamentary manipulation, but through the innovation and sheer determination of the President.

And yet, for all of this, how history will judge him, in the main, is going to hang very heavily on how the war evolves and what it will be said, many years from now, was gained or lost in that conflict. It is sometimes argued that Vietnam wasn't everything, that the American commitment didn't begin with Lyndon Johnson anyway, that the great domestic problems probably would not have been dealt with, let alone disposed of, much differently if there had been no great expansion of the war in the Johnson years. Perhaps. But the fact remains that Vietnam was, of course, the thing that seemed to be the well-spring of dissent, the issue that shook public confidence, the great preoccupation of the top men of government, the spoiler of relationships with allies and antagonists abroad, and the crisis that brought Lyndon Johnson down. There were other sources of dissent, other spoilers; there would have been trouble anyway because there always is trouble enough somewhere, growing out of something or other, for any President. But it was always President Johnson's firm belief that a Government which lost its mastery over Congress, and in the process lost the faith of the people, on one critical issue, was in grave danger of losing its capacity to command support or trust in anything it touched. This, in a sense, is what happened to Lyndon Johnson with Vietnam, and it happened because the President never managed until much too late to reconcile what he was trying to accomplish in the war, first with what the military men were trying to accomplish, and then with what the public thought he was trying to accomplish. He did not lead, or educate or rally the country until it was too late.

And so the dissent grew and the war dragged on and finally it had to be conceded, if not acknowledged publicly, that pouring on more pressure and projecting the possibility of an ever-widening, open-ended war was not going to compel the enemy to stop doing what it was doing, in Dean Rusk's phrase. Finally, it had to be conceded that there were limits to this new thing called limited war, and while this is progress of a kind it is not quite the same thing as success.

It is often said of Mr. Johnson that his trouble came from some incapacity to inspire, and thus to lead. He would say, on the contrary, that he was unjustly victimized by Easterners and intellectuals and liberals and the Kennedy people who scorned him for his regionalism and his roughness, his table manners and the twang of his voice. There is truth to both, and also irony, because the sad thing is that his origins are the best thing about him, the thing he has going for him whenever he is himself, and he didn't know it. Or maybe he just wasn't confident enough about it. Whatever it was, he tried to run the country in the way he ran the United States Senate and it didn't work. He wheedled and cajoled and high-pressured and over-sold, and seemed to be counting the legislation passed not so much for its contents as its bulk, and this wasn't what people were concerned about. They were worrying about casualty figures and about how the combat troops got to Vietnam in the first place and how they got involved in combat operations when the Secretaries of State and Defense had said they weren't supposed to; they were worrying about how it was all going to end and what it was doing to the country and whether it was worth it, and by the time the Administration got around to leveling a little more on the subject it was too late, because the confidence was gone.

This isn't the whole story by any means but it was a big part of the story of how Lyndon Johnson lost his majority. If he was like Lincoln, a sad man, he didn't show it and he didn't let it slow him; he was forever driving. He wanted nothing more than to succeed—and he did, in many, many ways. But he wanted support for the war and money for a bigger antipoverty effort and safety in the streets and housing for the poor and education for all our children and medical care for all the elderly and the love and respect of all the people, and it wouldn't stretch. He wanted to get it all at once and Roosevelt was right: nobody can.

Do You, Governor Kirk?

(AUGUST 3, 1970)

(for editorials supporting peaceful desegregation)

HORANCE G. DAVIS, JR.
Gainesville (Fla.) *Sun*

HORANCE DAVIS, JR., said he wrote his Pulitzer-winning editorials "past midnight with two fingers on the typewriter." The prize was awarded for a campaign consisting of more than 30 editorials calling for peaceful desegregation of Florida's schools. The editorials argued that desegregation could be accomplished without violence. When violence did occur, Davis said, editorials in the *Gainesville Sun* "promptly deplored it." The focal point of editorial criticism was politicians who opposed busing whites to achieve racial balance in the schools. "We took the position that this was a lot of horseradish," Davis said, "and that we had been busing whites past Negro schools for years." The object of attack in the editorial below was Florida's Governor Claude Kirk.

GOVERNOR Claude Kirk is due in Gainesville today, and we want to pose a question.

Does he want re-election so badly that he will pull a George Wallace and split Florida's people asunder?

It is a fair question, we think, because of Governor Kirk's racial posture of the past few months. Early this year, he sought extension of the deadline for school desegregation. This was not unreasonable.

But what followed was contemptible. He descended into Manatee County, twice suspended the School Board to keep it from implementing court orders, and caused a confrontation with U.S. marshals almost to the point of violence. Under threat of contempt of court and $10,000 daily fine, Governor Kirk retreated while muttering "victory" all the while.

Victory for whom? Certainly not law and order.

The governor's latest binge concerns private schools. He attacked the U.S. Revenue Service for removing their tax exemptions. Governor Kirk conveniently ignores that the IRS ruling clearly applies only to segregation academies.

155

Does Kirk approve of federal tax exemptions to schools created to avoid integration? "I don't know of any school that is actually doing what you're saying," he replied.

We can give some tips.

—While he's in Alachua County today, Governor Kirk might chat with County Commissioner Ralph Cellon, whose Rolling Green Academy out Alachua way was founded after school integration in February, has 100 students, a faculty of 7, and tuition of $450.

—He might also look into the explosive expansion of the Heritage Christian School out on North 34th Street, which intruded on public property to recruit students who had the necessary $575.

—He might ask about the embryonic Oak Hall Preparatory School founded by Dr. Billy Brashear and Dr. Harry L. Walker, open to all "without regard to race, creed or color"—with $1,100 tuition, of course.

These are not monumental and hardly worth pressing. More important is the state of Claude Kirk's mind. And we desire to address him directly.

Back in 1964 when passions ran hot, you said this, Governor Kirk: "I believe in equality before the law and equality of opportunity. . . . We must put to an end the cultivated feeling of minorities and recognize that we are all Americans."

Back in 1967, you told the *Saturday Evening Post:* "I'm not one of those red-necked governors like Lester Maddox. . . . I'm the only good guy in the South."

Later, when invited to a segregation conference in Alabama, you said: "We here in Florida . . . cannot join in attempts to subvert or delay the law of the land as interpreted by the Supreme Court."

The important thing, Governor Kirk, is whether you have abandoned these high ideals and cast your political lot on the side of bigotry.

Do you, Governor Kirk, think so little of your people?

Whitewash

(JANUARY 21, 1971)

(for editorials during 1970)

JOHN STROHMEYER

Bethlehem (Pa.) *Globe-Times*

IN August of 1970, Bethlehem, Pennsylvania, experienced the first episode in what became a continuing series of gang violence arising from racial tension. In the first outburst, a 14-year-old girl was killed and a 16-year-old boy seriously wounded at a neighborhood youth center. The city council ordered the youth center closed, and the mayor called for a police crackdown on youths congregating in the area. Confrontations resulted, and a number of youths considered troublemakers by the police were beaten. The director of the youth center, blamed for the troubles by much of the city, was charged with conspiracy. In January of 1971, a young patrolman, John Stein, resigned and charged police with inviting confrontations and the chief of police with making a point of participating in one beating. The city council refused to investigate the charges. During all this time, John Strohmeyer, editor of the the *Bethlehem Globe-Times,* questioned the actions of police and city government. In June the charges against the director of the youth center were dropped after a legal defense fund had been started for him. Eventually, the youth center was reopened, the police department took steps to correct its procedures, programs were begun to improve community relations, and the director of the youth center was named Bethlehem's Outstanding Young Man of the Year by the Junior Chamber of Commerce. Below is Strohmeyer's editorial challenging the city council's failure to investigate police beatings after the resignation of Patrolman Stein.

THE vote of confidence passed by City Council to reaffirm its faith in the Bethlehem police force is about as meaningless as a vote for motherhood. It was an obvious attempt to apply a coat of whitewash on important issues raised by the concerns of former policeman John Stein.

Ex-officer Stein, who served on the force two and a half years, might have found it easier to step out silently and concentrate on his studies at Lehigh, where he is completing his fourth year. However, the cover-up of the role of high police officials in the station house beatings and the growing needless alienation between police and youth compelled him to state his views and risk the scorn of many of his former colleagues.

Only Councilmen William J. P. Collins and Walter Dealtrey seemed to understand the issues raised by Stein's account: (1) How could a departmental hearing which recommended a verbal reprimand really deal with the matter when, as it now develops, Public Safety Director Irvin Good was seen swinging at one of the youths corralled in the police station on the night of September 25? Was Good identified as a participant, and, if so, was he supposed to reprimand himself? (2) There have been many police arrests but few cases ever get to the prosecution stage: Why? As Councilman Collins asked, "I would like to know whether any of these alleged criminals have been given a license to commit crime?"

Council's blindness to these concerns was best expressed in the long harangue delivered by Councilman Ray Dietz who attempted to impugn the motives of John Stein, the *Globe-Times,* and apparently anyone else who would dare to question the operations of the Bethlehem police force. It never occurred to him that the motivations might have been public interest. Instead of recognizing his own public duty to clear the stigma, he chose to pour on platitudes about his pride in the police force. In the words of Mark Twain, Councilman Dietz showed only he would rather be popular than right.

A more proper way to "stand behind our police" is to ensure a responsible administration, to correct those abuses of police procedure which are letting so many arrest cases slip away, and to set standards for the vast majority of city policemen who want to do their duty above reproach.

By voting not to clear the air, City Council indicated that it either doubts its own ability to muster "a calm and serious approach" to the truth, or it is so certain of the outcome of an investigation that it fears the revelations.

Our $213 Million Gift Horse
(MARCH 17, 1972)

(for editorials during 1972)

ROGER B. LINSCOTT
Berkshire Eagle (Pittsfield, Mass.)

IN the Pulitzer awards for editorial writing in the 1970s, an emphasis on local political and social issues was prominent. Roger Linscott wrote about local conditions in a way that prompted the Pulitzer personnel to remark that there "isn't anything very bland about [his] editorials." Employing a combination of sharp criticism, humor, irony and sarcasm along with fact and analysis, Linscott focused on a number of targets—not without some effect. His editorials castigating two hospital boards for refusing to participate in a family planning project resulted in one hospital changing its position. After several critical editorials on local bus service, the city council in Pittsfield, Massachusetts, the home of Linscott's *Berkshire Eagle,* set up a commission to study ways to improve the service. Included here is one of the editorials Linscott wrote opposing the wasteful spending of $213 million on local highways. In it, he contends that other needs were more important, even though they might take away federal money from his area. Following Linscott's criticism, the highway project was dropped.

WHEN liberal academic types complain that this nation is suffering from a badly distorted sense of political priorities, the complaint is often cast in such abstract terms that it doesn't really register.

But we now have a concrete locally oriented example of what they're talking about, in the form of the state's proposal to allocate $213 million of interstate highway funds to a revamping of Routes 7 and 8 here in Berkshire County.

Nobody in these parts, of course, is likely to object very strenuously to such an outpouring of federal largesse. It would be nice to have a super-road to hustle transients through the area and to give all parts of the county speedier access to the Massachusetts Turnpike. And there is always the rationalization that if the Berkshires don't get the money some other area will.

159

Nonetheless, $213 million is a staggering sum of money. And at the risk of seeming to look a gift horse in the mouth, it is tempting to consider some of the other things that such a sum could buy.

For instance, with $213 million you could clean up the Housatonic River from its tributaries in Windsor to the Connecticut border, with probably enough left over to create recreational ponds and parks along its course.

Or you could build and equip enough schools to take care of all of the county's public educational needs for the next decade.

Or, if you wanted to dole out the $213 million to the cities and towns of the Berkshires as a revenue sharing device, it would be sufficient to permit a total moratorium on all local real estate taxes, throughout the county, for a period of about 10 years.

Or, to carry it from the sublime to the ridiculous, as a direct per capita hand-out it would be enough to provide a cash payment of nearly $3,000 apiece to every one of the county's 70,000-odd adult inhabitants.

But none of these purposes, worthy or otherwise, can have any claim on the federal money. The highway lobby has long since seen to that. The $213 million (more precisely, 90 per cent of it) would come from the federal Highway Trust Fund, which is lavishly nourished by the federal gas tax and is earmarked by law exclusively for highway purposes.

Indeed, as things now stand the Highway Trust Fund's multibillion dollar cornucopia can't even be applied to alternative forms of public transportation, despite the fact that a decent mass transit system in this country would serve to lighten the burden on our highways and save our cities from strangulation at the hands of the motor car. Just this week, Transportation Secretary John Volpe asked Congress for permission to spend a portion of the fund on mass transit in the coming fiscal year—and the best bet on Capitol Hill is that the answer will be no.

In the case of the Berkshires, the plan is to make available for Routes 7 and 8 most of the money the federal authorities had allocated to the Boston area but which isn't being spent there because of the governor's moratorium on new highway construction within the Route 128 circle. Because of the lower land-taking costs in the hinterlands, the state highway planners figure they can build 66 miles of super-road in the Berkshires for what a mere 4 miles would cost in the congested Boston area. This, they point out, is quite a bargain.

No doubt it is, if measured solely in miles of concrete. And no doubt, if the money has to be spent somewhere and can be spent on highway construction only we should welcome it. But there's no law against wishing for a system in which urgent social needs might be able to take fiscal priority over the inexhaustible demands of the automobile.

Mr. Cahill's Colleagues
(APRIL 10, 1973)

(for editorials on scandals in state government)

F. GILMAN SPENCER
Trenton (N. J.) *Trentonian*

IN 1973 the issue of government corruption came to a head. In Washington the presidential administration of Richard Nixon was mired in the Watergate scandal. Across the nation came charges of political impropriety. In New Jersey revelations of state officials' misdeeds piled up on top of each other. For years the state had been plundered by its politicians. Finally, its secretary of state was convicted of bribery. Then its attorney general was accused of attempting to cover up the secretary's crime. When the State Investigations Commission exonerated the attorney general, it was charged with a whitewash. Numerous officials were accused of misuse of government equipment and corruption in campaign fund-raising. For the governor, William T. Cahill, the charges were especially damaging if for no other reason than the fact that in 1973 he was running for reelection. Continually focusing public attention on the scandals was F. Gilman Spencer, editor of the *Trentonian* in Trenton. His editorials are immediately distinguishable among Pulitzer winners for their free use of flippant phrasing. Of the suggestion that a legislative investigating committee be appointed, Spencer wrote: "Just the thought of Democrats and Republicans, many of whom couldn't care less about official corruption or personal reputation, joining in such an election year battle, is enough to send one into the streets, naked and screaming." Of one scandal he declared: "Even the most pious, biased, know-nothing Republican vegetable this side of Saturn should find it worthy of his attention." Another scandal was so "gorgeously simple that a reasonably alert farm animal would have little trouble grasping [its] significance." One government program, Spencer claimed, "could have been more competently conducted by a wayward garter snake than it was by the State of New Jersey." In time, a number of the state's officials were convicted of misdeeds, the State Investigations Commission was discredited, and Cahill lost his governorship to Democrat Brendan Byrne. In the editorial reprinted here, Spencer attempts to explain details of some of the corruption and point out their political significance.

161

So-CALLED political corruption scandals have a way of throwing a lot of semi-recognizable names at you and defying you to make one whit's worth of sense out of them or the incredibly complicated charges attached to them. Thus, the undoubtedly diminutive segment of the public that is struggling to understand the alleged Cahill election campaign financing scandal could be forgiven at this point if it were simply to throw up its hands and say to hell with it.

Even the most average of average New Jerseyans has a pretty good idea who Governor William T. Cahill is. But don't expect too much from Mr. Average when you start tossing out names like Paul Sherwin . . . Bruce Mahon . . . Eugene Mori . . . William Colsey . . . Joseph McCrane. And expect even less when those names are followed by the weirdo charge that untold thousands in Cahill campaign contribution checks were cashed at Garden State Park . . . yes, that's right, at the race track.

That's why this particular editorial isn't directed at Mr. Average or even at Mr. Slightly Above Average. This editorial is for one man and one man alone—a man who will intimately appreciate the significance of the names and the allegations. His name is Cahill. His current objective is to get himself reelected. His problem is that a bunch of his good friends and close political associates keep popping up in the damndest places . . . like on the front pages of newspapers and smack in the middle of criminal investigations.

We are not going to waste our time repeating all the nice things we and others have said about many of the fine things Mr. Cahill has accomplished as Governor. Nor are we going to point out once again the disaster that could befall us all if the campaign thing or a couple of other dark episodes involving Cahill people were to result in the election of a Charley Sandman or a Ralph DeRose, neither of whom is fit to run a rat-judging contest, let alone the State of New Jersey. What must be said now, however, and said plainly, is that too many people too close to the Governor have been accused of doing too many things that have a way of destroying reputations of administrative purity.

We say this in full knowledge of the newness and incompleteness of the latest charges, which have yet to be confirmed by anyone really worth listening to. If the Garden State affair were the only thing to have called Cahill cohorts into question, we would be writing an entirely different sort of editorial or none at all.

But Mr. Cahill's number two man, Secretary of State Paul Sherwin, was convicted of bribery-conspiracy. A top GOP fund-raiser for the Cahill campaign, William Loughran, was also convicted in the same case. According to testimony at Sherwin's trial, a $10,000 kickback was handed to William Colsey, another Cahill fund-raiser, in the presence of New Jersey Treasurer Joseph McCrane, outside his State House office.

Mr. McCrane is the son-in-law of Eugene Mori, owner of Garden State Park race track. Mr. Mori is said to own a large tract of land adjacent to the huge new sports complex, proposed by the Cahill administration and now under construction in New Jersey. Mr. McCrane, a close personal friend of the Governor who recently resigned as State Treasurer, has allegedly been implicated in the campaign financing situation, as has another close political associate of the Governor, Bruce Mahon, Burlington County GOP figure and real estate broker, who, with Mr. Cahill, was blasted for land speculation deals by Democratic gubernatorial candidate Robert Meyner during the 1969 campaign. Cahill and Mahon denied the charges.

Another Cahill Administration official—Attorney General George Kugler—was recently absolved of attempting to cover-up the Sherwin case, but only after an investigation agency completely discounted the testimony of two top federal prosecutors.

Regardless of how one chooses to view all this, it is a fact that several top-echelon Cahill confederates have troubles the Governor doesn't need, particularly in an election year. It is also a fact that Mr. Cahill has not always reacted to charges involving men close to him in a way that fully inspires public confidence.

Obviously, there are ways to deal with the indelicate situation which now confronts him. But there are few ways he can deal with it without attacking his own. Whether Mr. Cahill will pay that price or can afford to is one of the largest questions to be asked in New Jersey in years.

Where They Square Off
and
Washington, the Father or an Infamous Traitor?

(for editorials on a schoolbook controversy)

JOHN DANIELL MAURICE
Charleston (W. Va.) *Daily Mail*

WHEN the schools of Kanawha County, West Virginia, became the center of a public protest over textbooks, the county had an editor ably suited to explain the controversy. John Daniell Maurice, editor of the *Charleston Daily Mail,* years before had won the Sigma Delta Chi editorial writing award for his opposition to the mayor's efforts to ban the book *Peyton Place* from the local library. The textbook dispute focused on works containing writings by such figures as the poet Allen Ginsberg and Black Panther Eldridge Cleaver. At one point, feelings ran so strong that attempts were made to force the closing of the public schools. Throughout the controversy, Maurice, generally disagreeing with the protestors, provided a keen analysis and remained admirably fair in his commentary. He felt the textbooks were simply a salient target for popular indignation over certain trends in education. The deeper complaints of protestors, Maurice suggested, were that public schools no longer were teaching traditional values, that they had abandoned "patriotism" for "social change," and that they were not neutral but hostile toward religion. Perhaps because Maurice helped to provide a calmer atmosphere to study the problem, protestors agreed to have the courts settle the dispute, and the board of education, agreeing that protestors had not been allowed any input into selection of textbooks, finally withdrew much of the objectionable material and set up new guidelines and procedures for selecting texts. Reprinted here are two editorials, from nearly fifty Maurice wrote during the controversy, demonstrating his balanced analysis of the fundamentals of the dispute.

WHERE THEY SQUARE OFF
(OCTOBER 16, 1974)

MOST of the "fundamentalists" we talk to in this textbook controversy are utterly convincing on one point: They have no objection to the school curriculum which maintains toward religion, the churches and their spiritual and moral values a strict neutrality. In their dedication to the First Amendment, freedom of worship and the separation of church and state, they are as respectful as anyone.

The "fundamentalist" objection is this: That in the guise of a benevolent neutrality toward faith and its religious expression, the public schools are imposing upon the young and the impressionable something called "humanism," which is not neutral at all. On the contrary, it is a counter-religion of its own which is often hostile to and even subversive of the traditional beliefs and values and enjoys in this ageless struggle between faith and disbelief the overwhelming advantage of the political authority.

Most of the "humanists" we talk to in this textbook controversy are utterly blind and deaf to this objection. Like the "fundamentalists" in their faith, the "humanists" in their conviction cannot acknowledge as a fact or admit as a possibility that there is any antithesis. Let the churches teach one thing (on Sunday), the public schools everything else (Monday through Friday), and in this neat division of time and subject there is nothing to worry about.

The Roman Catholic Church knows better. Almost from the beginning, it has known that the schools which do not teach religion by design teach something else by default. It could be atheism, agnosticism, hedonism, scientism or, as the "fundamentalists" insist, "humanism," but in any case it is non- and potentially anti-religious.

Thus the Catholics have never readily conceded the possibility of education apart from the Church. "Pluralism," which currently enjoys a great vogue, is an invention of the "humanists." And where the church is not a full partner with the state in the education of the young, it does what it does in the United States. It exercises its constitutional option to maintain its own schools and teach and train as it pleases. Not at all incidentally, that option is also a "humanist" invention.

One word may illuminate the profound difference. For the true believer a miracle is no mystery. It is simply God's handiwork. For the "humanist" it is simply something science hasn't yet fully explained and surely will as soon as it gets around to it.

It is a genuine and enduring impasse in the controversy over texts and subject matter, and we describe it sketchily not from any knowledge of how it may be avoided or finessed. Rather it is to point out the probable consequences of persisting in the attack.

One is the destruction of the public school system as the American people have known it for more than a century. Another is the substitution of a conglomerate of private schools—as many as may be required to give full expression in education to the great variety of religious and anti-religious conviction.

WASHINGTON, THE FATHER OR AN INFAMOUS TRAITOR?
(DECEMBER 7, 1974)

GENERALLY, there are two distinct philosophies on how to bring up the child so that in maturity he does not make a nuisance of himself.

The first and older of the two relies heavily upon training. Train the child. Train him so that when he grows up he will find his values, attitudes, even his habits ready-made for him. He will behave thereafter as he has been trained or indoctrinated to behave.

The second and more modern shifts the emphasis to education. Educate the child so that when he grows up he can think for himself and shape those values, attitudes and habits which serve him best in a rapidly changing environment.

Now this is a schematic distinction which clearly does not apply in the practice. The choice is not an "either-or." But one example, drawn from the textbook controversy, will suffice to illustrate the dispute over emphasis.

Most Americans have been brought up to esteem patriotism as the hallmark of their citizenship and good fortune. They were brought up, or trained, in this value because their parents and teachers wanted it that way. They wanted a generation of Americans conditioned to loyalty and duty. They did not want a generation educated to think freely about the conflicting values of patriotism and disloyalty and fall by error into the latter.

The mechanics of this indoctrination are familiar to everyone—the Pledge of Allegiance, the National Anthem, the salute to the flag. At this command decision, students are not educated to think it through and decide for themselves whether George Washington was, indeed, the Father of his Country or as millions of loyal Englishmen thought of him, the worst traitor to the crown since Oliver Cromwell. They learned the answer before they were old enough to think about it.

And at bottom, this is what the textbook wrangle is all about. Not to train the child in the values his parents have found enduring is to neglect him. Not to educate him is to condemn him to repetitious ignorance.

What is needed is an agreement upon the right mixture, and when this is reached the controversy will disappear.

Justice Is Blind—and Gagged

(NOVEMBER 26, 1975)

1976

(for editorials against government secrecy and judicial censorship)

PHILIP P. KERBY
Los Angeles Times

FOR the fourth time in the history of the Pulitzer Prizes, the award for editorial writing in 1976 was given for editorials on freedom of the press. The subjects of attack for Phil Kerby were primarily legislation and judicial decisions restricting publication of information. (Coincidentally, the *Los Angeles Times'* first Pulitzer Prize for Meritorious Public Service in 1942 was for a defense of freedom of the press.) The majority of Phil Kerby's editorials dealt with press "gag orders" issued by trial judges and proposed federal legislation for stricter control over information relating to "national defense." Both topics were of major concern to the press in 1975. While Kerby provides some persuasive, clearly stated arguments against both restrictions, his reasoning is one-sided and his predictions sometimes exaggerated, not an unusual approach for journalists to take when discussing freedom of the press. In denouncing, for example, what he saw as a "radical trend in the courts toward censorship," he argues cogently that the "courts, agents of the people, have no proprietary right to dispense as little or as much news about their proceedings as they wish. Judges do not own the news." On the other hand, when the First and Fifth Amendments are both involved, there is little doubt in Kerby's editorials of which should take priority and no room for defenses of a right to a "fair" trial. In one editorial, Kerby even criticizes courts for overturning criminal convictions because of prejudicial publicity. A small degree of inconsistency occasionally shows also from under the cloak of objective analysis. In one editorial, for example, Kerby criticizes as an intrusion into privacy a law that opened information on bank accounts (without divulging depositors' names) to the Internal Revenue Service, while in another he denounces a privacy bill that would have shielded personal information from public disclosure by the press. Reprinted here is Kerby's most frequently mentioned editorial discussing the widening tendency of judges to restrict more and more information.

THIS country may be moving toward secret trials. United States Supreme Court Justice Harry A. Blackmun's ruling in a Nebraska mass murder case points in that direction.

Justice Blackmun, upholding in part a "gag" order imposed by a Nebraska judge, decided that courts may forbid the news media to report confessions and other incriminating evidence before trial even though such information has been disclosed at a public hearing.

The original gag order by a Nebraska district court judge was comprehensive, but Blackmun's ruling went farther. The district court order prohibited the press from reporting details of the arrest of a suspect, the identity of a victim or victims who had been sexually assaulted, the results of ballistics and medical tests and the facts of a confession or the fact there had been a confession. Moreover, the court said "the exact nature of the limitations of publicity as entered by this order will not be reported," barring the media from reporting the extent of the censorship.

Justice Blackmun lifted the Nebraska judge's restrictions on reporting the details of the crime and the identities of the victims, but then reaffirmed the court's right to impose censorship by saying, "At the same time, I cannot and do not, at least on an application for a stay and at this distance, impose a prohibition upon the Nebraska courts from placing any restrictions at all upon what the media may report prior to trial."

Of more ominous significance, Justice Blackmun went on to lay down the procedures of censorship. He said, "The accused, and the prosecution if it joins him, bears the burden of showing that publicizing particular facts will irreparably impair the ability of those exposed to them to reach an independent and impartial judgment as to guilt."

This part of Blackmun's opinion is a transparent rationale for suppression, a mere admonition to the courts to go through a ritualistic exercise before imposing censorship. To say that a burden must be met is to say that it can be met and that prior restraint of publication can be imposed and backed by the use of the contempt power. Prior restraint always has been regarded as repugnant to the First Amendment. Briefly imposed in the Pentagon Papers case, it fell even though the government argued that publication would cause an immediate and irreparable threat to national security.

Blackmun accepted without reservation the theory that prospective jurors must be delivered to a courtroom in pristine innocence. He phrased it this way: "A prospective juror who has read or heard of the confession . . . may well be unable to form an independent judgment as to guilt or innocence from the evidence adduced at trial."

The presumption here is that once a prospective juror reads or hears about a pending case, the juror instantly decides the guilt or innocence of the defendant and becomes from then on an automaton. This view of jurors was expressed in a crescendo of condescending words by a defense attorney in a celebrated California trial four years ago. He said, "Miss [Angela] Davis was presumed guilty from the moment her name appeared in the press. . . . One would have to be blind, deaf, dumb and dishonest to say that the articles I have quoted will not and have not affected the impartiality of potential jurors."

This argument was marred only by one flaw. It was not true. The jury returned a not-guilty verdict, and that has been the outcome of a series of trials in recent years in which jurors were said to be predisposed toward conviction by publicity.

Blackmun said in the Nebraska case that once trial starts restrictions on information should be removed, but it is only a step from suppressing information in open, pre-trial proceedings to censoring the trial itself.

If this view is considered extreme, a look at the record shows otherwise. At first the courts tested their powers by placing restrictions only on those within the system—prosecutors and defense attorneys—forbidding them to discuss prejudicial matters outside the courtroom. Gag orders were then extended to the media. A Los Angeles judge, caught up in an excess of zeal, banned comment about a case by the chief of police and the mayor. Another zealot on the Los Angeles bench ordered that nothing could be reported about a murder case except information heard in court. He was reversed, and so was a New York judge who banned the public from an extortion trial and conducted it in secret, but the trend in the courts toward secrecy is strong.

Secrecy was invoked in the New York case, as it is invoked in all court censorship, in behalf of a fair trial, but justice is not a private affair, and the best assurance of justice is to keep the courts, and all other public institutions, under public surveillance.

This issue is not between the courts and primarily the press. It is between censorious judges and the public. Secrecy lays no burden upon the press, which is only the intermediary, the messenger. The censorship that is imposed is censorship on the public. It is the public that the ministers of justice hold in contempt.

Conforte's Influence

•

Conforte Influence in Washoe County Is Shocking

•

Reno's Reputation

(for editorials challenging power of a local brothel keeper)

FOSTER CHURCH, NORMAN F. CARDOZA,
and WARREN L. LERUDE
Nevada State Journal and *Reno Evening Gazette*

JOE CONFORTE opened his house of prostitution in the 1950s just across the county line from Reno, Nevada. From there he began to service the Reno metropolitan area. Because prostitution is legal in Nevada, Conforte's activities were accepted, and soon he was dropping money into the area's worthiest charities. A colorful character, he got and welcomed nationwide attention. Conforte's interests, though, were not limited to prostitution and charity. He clandestinely consorted with local politicians, passing out money and the services of his prostitutes, gaining for himself favorable treatment in his real estate dealings. The *Nevada State Journal* and the *Reno Evening Gazette* began to shed light on Conforte's political activities and the acceptance he had received from even such groups as the YMCA. As editorials by Warren Lerude, executive editor, Foster Church, editorial page editor of the *Journal,* and Norman Cardoza, *Gazette* editorial page editor, hit home, Conforte fought back with denouncements of the papers and many area citizens criticized the editorial treatment Conforte was receiving. While the papers were sometimes criticized for attempting to attract circulation by their frequent use of the word "whorehouse" and their page one coverage of Conforte's activities, the newspapers continued their assault. Eventually Conforte took on a low profile, politicians began avoiding him, and charities announced they would no longer accept his contributions. The editorials reprinted here criticize the notoriety achieved by Conforte.

Conforte's Influence
(MARCH 17, 1976)
Foster Church

IT is a measure of the times that Joe Conforte is one of the two or three best known citizens of Washoe County. Conforte has achieved a sort of folk character status since arriving in this area and opening his house of prostitution.

Several articles concerning Conforte have appeared in national publications. His personal style—vulgar and overstated—has made him highly visible whether he is seen driving his custom automobile or arriving at a sporting event, attired in expensive clothing and accompanied by women, reputedly prostitutes from his Mustang Ranch.

Popular literature and movies glorify the anti-hero. Conforte, who appears to have made his fortune by himself in an unconventional business, is regarded by some members of the community with a certain affection.

The report of the Washoe County Grand Jury that details the influence which Conforte has wielded over at least five public officials reveals the real Conforte: A man who is ambitious for power, influence and money, a man who does not hesitate to seduce public officials by offering them food, drink, money, airplane flights and the services of prostitutes. He is a man who, despite well-publicized gifts to the community, is intent on shrewd business deals and currying the influence of public officials to amass even more money.

The grand jury report details quite exhaustively Conforte's apparently successful attempts to make a killing on a land deal. Virtually nothing of Conforte's involvement in the deal was revealed to the public. Conforte worked behind the scenes. And if the Washoe County Convention Authority goes ahead with its plan to develop a golf course on property purchased from him, he could make more than $1 million.

It should be plain to anyone reading the report that Conforte, while he has done nothing illegal, has morally corrupted some public officials. And public officials appear to have profited in a variety of ways from their association with him.

The group that has obviously not profited by their association is the public which these officials promised to serve.

Reading the report, there are signs from the time the Capurro-Gault property was said to be for sale, that the public has lost out continuously to Conforte's manipulations.

In February of 1973, the Capurro-Gault land was for sale for $5,000 an acre. Sparks City Councilman Gordon Foote made a motion that the Sparks City Council go on record as being in favor of buying the land.

Sparks Councilmen James Vernon and Pete Lemberes voted against the motion. A month later, the property was snapped up by Conforte.

Soon after the purchase, Vernon and Lemberes attempted to influence the city of Sparks to buy the land from Conforte and develop it as a golf course. Failing this, Vernon, Lemberes and Washoe County Commissioner Gerry Grow attempted to influence the Convention Authority to buy the land and develop it.

Shown that the Convention Authority would not be able to finance both the golf course and a proposed addition to Centennial Coliseum, Grow and Vernon proposed an increase in the room tax collected in the Reno-Sparks area.

And when it appeared the convention authority might be expanded to include four new members, then state Senator Stan Drakulich appeared before the convention authority to oppose the proposal. Drakulich had previously received $18,000 from Conforte as a real estate commission for the Capurro-Gault land transaction. He has acknowledged he did virtually nothing to earn the commission.

The increased room tax was approved with the support of Reno City Councilman Clyde Biglieri. Biglieri had already received a $20,000 commission from Conforte, according to the grand jury report, and could have profited handsomely by potential real estate sales when Conforte developed the land around the golf course.

And according to the grand jury report, while all this was taking place, Grow, Lemberes and Vernon were frequent visitors to Mustang Ranch. They discussed the public's business with Conforte. They were offered food, drink and the services of prostitutes. According to the report they even discussed getting rid of Reno Mayor Sam Dibitonto because he opposed the room tax increase.

The land transaction is only one example of Conforte's wide-ranging clandestine influence in area politics. According to the report, he was in a position to at least exert influence in the choice of a Reno police chief. And his political contributions, numerous and frequently large, have been accepted, and usually concealed by public officials ashamed of the associations with him.

When the veneer of the folk hero is stripped from Conforte, he becomes simply another man who desires to make large profits. He uses public officials to accomplish his ends. We see no indication that the public welfare enters his considerations.

Perhaps the public is partially at fault for having viewed Conforte with affection and amusement. But his influence, if it continues, should be open to public scrutiny.

Officials who became a part of his web of influence and have not yet been exposed should come forward now and admit it. They will probably be revealed eventually. The onus of being exposed later will be worse than voluntary disclosure.

No one can forbid an official to associate with Conforte but the association should not be clandestine. A secret meeting with a brothel owner cannot be in the public's interest. But as the grand jury report has shown, a brothel owner can profit handsomely by such dealings.

Conforte Influence in Washoe County Is Shocking
(march 17, 1976)
Norman F. Cardoza

Nevadans who believe that brothel operator Joe Conforte's influence in government affairs in this county have been blown out of proportion should read the county grand jury's new report on his relationship with various local officials.

It is flabbergasting. It confirms some of the rumors circulating for years that Conforte does indeed work hard and effectively at getting local and state officials into his influence.

It made many startling revelations, among them the following:

—That Conforte gave money to Washoe County Commissioner Gerry Grow for his election campaign, and offered Grow free services at the Conforte brothel.

—That Conforte also gave campaign money to Reno Mayor Carl Bogart and Councilman Clyde Biglieri. Other public officials received Conforte campaign money, too, the report intimates. They were not the object of this particular investigation and were not named.

—That Conforte lobbied various officials, some of whom he favored with campaign funds, to gather support for his golf course land deal near Sparks. This transaction, according to the jury testimony, stood to make him a million dollars.

—That he also lobbied officials to swing an increase in the county room tax in order to generate the public tax money necessary to bring the project to fruition.

—That he offered free food, drink and prostitute services to former Sparks Councilmen Pete Lemberes and Jim Vernon, both of whom were also in a position to help in boosting the golf course project.

—That he bought the 344 acres through the real estate firm owned by Biglieri and that Biglieri personally realized a $20,000 commission from the sale.

—That terms of sale dictated by Conforte awarded $18,000 of the

$86,000 commission money to then state Senator Stan Drakulich for no reason that has been revealed.

—That he chartered a private plane to fly Grow back to Washoe County from Washington state, where he and his family were vacationing, in order for Grow to sign sale papers for a County Convention Authority golf course land purchase from Conforte.

—That he paid Grow's airline fare back to Washington and that he gave the commissioner $100 for his inconvenience.

—That he tried to have Councilman Lemberes's brother, Alex, appointed as Reno chief of police when a vacancy occurred.

—That he tried to talk former Reno Mayor Sam Dibitonto into accepting his choices for some Reno appointive positions. (Dibitonto, the jury found, refused to do so).

The most eye-opening aspect of the report is the indication that Conforte not only tried, but was successful, in drawing various elected officials into his seine of influence.

Under questioning, Biglieri admitted having taken Conforte campaign money. Bigliere's firm did handle the land deal and the councilman did get half its $40,000 commission, Biglieri did represent the tie-breaking vote on the council necessary to pass the room tax increase that in turn was necessary to make the golf course project possible.

Grow has admitted flying south to sign the papers, thus saving Conforte thousands of dollars in interest payments. He has admitted taking Conforte campaign money and the $100 gift. And he does not deny that he, Vernon and Lemberes met on several occasions to talk business with Conforte at his brothel.

Bogart has denied receiving Conforte campaign contributions, but the grand jury report claims he did receive the funds.

The grand jury notes that none of this has involved criminal conduct, so far as is known. The state's new conflict of interest law was not in effect when much of it was going on, and the law is now being challenged in the courts.

But it disproves any idea that Conforte is in reality a harmless character whose interest in civic affairs in this area in recent years is benevolent.

In fact the report clearly spells out Conforte's design to lure public officialdom into his influence for the purpose of personal gain.

Given a chance, we believe, he would try to control local government. Imagine how the rest of the country would react to the news of a brothel owner running government in this gaming community.

What is more, it would give Conforte the opportunity to legalize prostitution in this county and that, for reasons we needn't enumerate, would be a problem.

The report, we believe, should also be of grave concern to the citizens of this county because of the conduct of the public officials involved.

Not only were they foolish in the extreme in getting involved with Conforte, but they acted reprehensibly in doing it clandestinely.

There'll be no conflict charges. The state conflict of interest law is in a state of limbo. But the conflict is nonetheless clear.

The trust that the voters of this area put in the officials involved has been betrayed.

The citizens of Washoe County have a responsibility to read it all for themselves in the full jury report published in the *Gazette* on Tuesday.

It's not light reading. The Conforte influence web is complex and widespread. It takes some hard study to sort it all out.

But the reading is worth it. It's disgusting and deplorable. And it should arouse demands that the officials involved be called on the carpet.

The *Gazette* will make recommendations on such appropriate action in a subsequent editorial—to be published Thursday.

RENO'S REPUTATION
(MARCH 25, 1976)
Warren L. Lerude

FOR decades, Reno was known as the divorce capital of the world.

That's a reputation the citizenry at large, businessmen, in particular, and appreciators of the Truckee Meadows as a good place to live have tried to live down.

In recent times, divorce has gotten to be legally acceptable in many other states and Reno has matured as a pleasant family tourism center and sprouting business environment, through the likes of warehousing [and] light manufacturing.

Now, however, Reno faces a new reputation problem, created by the frequently national and sometimes international brothel promotion of Joe Conforte, coupled with the links some public officials have with him.

At the same time the community is trying to attract tourism and business by showing Reno to be a city of good values, Reno is becoming known as a whorehouse town, the kind of city that thinks it's great to have Joe's place called home.

Not long ago, a foreign film crew was in Reno. Were they excited about filming the beauty of Lake Tahoe, the cosmopolitan and free lifestyles of Reno, the excitement of the state's legal gambling?

What really excited this film crew from Japan was Joe Conforte's whorehouse. That's what they wished to film for the multitudes of tourists back in Japan who one day might visit Reno—the whorehouse town.

Over the weekend, a tragic shooting occurred at Mustang. A world famous boxer lay dead in a pool of blood a few feet from the fortress-like structure and its big fence and guard towers.

Around the world the story went on high-speed news teletypes. It's news when a world famous person dies in gunfire. And it's news where that takes place—the whorehouse, the one Joe Conforte runs, the one so many people around Reno have tolerated for so long as "just another business."

"Just another business?" Conforte? He who Washoe County sheriff's deputies say called them "dogs" and who was quoted by lawmen as pointing to the dead boxer's corpse and saying "It's just a dead man . . . so what?"

If Reno wishes to continue to build the reputation it is getting as being home base for Joe Conforte and his brothel, a reputation the city deserves when some of its highest officials connect themselves with Conforte, the present course of action will continue.

Reno charities, organizations, politicians, businesses will continue to cater to Conforte.

But if Reno is to move forward now into a constructive and wholesome tourism future it should cast aside its relationships with Joe Conforte.

As this newspaper has stated before, if Conforte wishes to run a whorehouse, let him do it just as others do in Nevada without all the fanfare that is beginning to stigmatize Reno. The madams of the brothels are not the most widely known citizens of Elko, Winnemucca and Ely. It's about time Reno put Joe Conforte's ambitions in the same Nevada perspective.

It is time he got the message from a city too silent so far that Reno does not want him to ride in its parades, finance its bus lines, influence its politicians, be front row center as the gamblers celebrate him with the best show room tables.

As before, the question is: Who has guts enough in this city to declare Conforte persona non grata?

Harrah's?

Harolds?

John Ascuaga and his Sparks Nugget?

Charlie Mapes?

Public officials who don't have connections with Conforte?

The YMCA?

The Reno Rotary Club?

The United Way?

Service clubs?

The YWCA?

The Reno Service League?

St. Mary's Guild?

Any clergy person who might feel it inappropriate for his or her city to be known as a whorehouse town?

The Greater Reno Chamber of Commerce board of directors by name has had the courage to stand against Conforte's arrogance. The chamber backed up by the Washoe County Grand Jury, which was critical of Conforte power.

Who, now, cares enough about Reno to stand with these business men and women?

The means is simple—a resolution declaring that Conforte's influence in local government is bad for this city. Get the resolution to this newspaper. We will report the news.

The word will begin to get around the country, just as has Conforte's promotion of prostitution, just as has the bad name public officials have brought the city because of the relationships with Conforte.

And maybe Reno can start living down the whorehouse reputation our silent citizens have allowed Conforte to build.

A Good Decision on Libel
(NOVEMBER 9, 1977)

(for selected examples of her work)

MEG GREENFIELD
Washington Post

THE controversy over the selection of the 1978 winner of the Pulitzer Prize received as much attention as the winner did. The jury choice for the award was Paul Greenberg of the *Pine Bluff* (Ark.) *Commercial,* winner of the 1969 Prize. Greenberg's exhibit contained eight editorials on educational standards and quality in the schools of Pine Bluff and Arkansas. The Advisory Board rejected Greenberg and selected Meg Greenfield of the *Washington Post.* In the editorial reprinted here, Meg Greenfield attempts to explain why a court ruling in favor of the press in a libel suit was "useful and wise." The editorial is admirable for its calmness of discussion about an area in which the press sometimes seems loudly dogmatic. The opening and closing paragraphs are refreshing in their frankness. The middle paragraphs, the body of the editorial, however, are little more than a typically routine statement of press law known to most college journalism students and verbatim quotation from the court decision. In 1979 the United States Supreme Court overruled the Appeals Court decision discussed here by Miss Greenfield.

WE think we are not just being hypersensitive when we say that there seems to be a pretty big difference these days between the way the press responds to a court decision upholding its First Amendment freedoms—and the way everyone else responds. Well, almost everyone else. The point is that what looks to us like a guarantee of the personal space required to do our job increasingly looks to others like a structure of special privileges, perks and exemptions that put the press beyond the reach of normal obligations and restraints. Another such decision—this one concerning libel—was reached by a Federal Appeals Court in New York on Monday. And on the theory that there may not be unanimity on this thing (there wasn't even unanimity on the bench, the decision being 2 to 1), we will try to explain why we think the ruling was useful and wise.

The libel suit had been brought against CBS by former Army Lieutenant Colonel Anthony Herbert; he was the subject of a CBS program called "The Selling of Colonel Herbert," which questioned the veracity of some of the charges the disaffected colonel had been making about the military with whom he served in Vietnam. The case itself still has not been settled. What has been settled, unless Colonel Herbert decides to appeal the ruling to the Supreme Court, is this: It is off-limits to the plaintiff in a libel case to inquire into a journalist-defendant's thoughts and opinions at the time he was putting together the offending story in order to establish the journalist's motives. The lower court judge said Colonel Herbert's attorneys could make such inquiries of a producer of "The Selling of Colonel Herbert." The Appeals Court said they could not.

The libel law, as it has been interpreted by the Supreme Court in its famous Sullivan decision and subsequent rulings, uses "malice" as the standard for determining liability. If you are a "public figure," as Colonel Herbert is, and you wish to establish that you have been libeled, you must prove that the defendant knew that a damaging statement was false or had reckless disregard for the truth or falsity of the statement—such as failing to try to verify the defamatory material in the face of serious doubts about its truthfulness. You must establish, in other words, that the defendant was acting in bad faith.

Clearly, then, on grounds of practicality and efficiency, there is an argument to be made for questioning the journalist-defendant about his motives. But there are strong reasons for ruling out this kind of inquiry and Judge Irving R. Kaufman, who wrote the Appeals Court's decision, made them. Judge Kaufman observed that the producer in question had provided a great deal of material for the plaintiff to review and had "answered innumerable questions about what he knew, or had seen; whom he had interviewed; intimate details of his discussions with interviewees; and the form and frequency of his communications with sources." But he had drawn the line at "a small number of questions relating to his beliefs, opinions, intent and conclusions in preparing the program." In pronouncing this line to have been the correct one, Judge Kaufman said that a court ruling otherwise would have been "condoning judicial review of the editor's thought processes. Such an inquiry, which on its face would be virtually boundless, endangers a constitutionally protected realm, and unquestionably puts a freeze on the free interchange of ideas within the newsroom."

It is, we will readily grant, easier to be in favor of a free and untrammeled press than it is to love the journalists who constitute it. In fact, we suspect that a lot of people would find it easier to swallow Judge Kaufman's opinion if it didn't mean also swallowing a measure of freedom and ease for a noisy, pushy, growly press. But that, alas, has something to do with the democratic condition. Sometimes you have to make choices. And the New York Appeals Court made the right one.

Solzhenitsyn at Harvard

(JUNE 11, 1978)

(for selected examples of his work)

EDWIN M. YODER

Washington Star

EDWIN M. YODER was not the first choice of the Pulitzer nominating committee. He shows in his work, though, an intellectual depth on a wide range of topics. A Phi Beta Kappa graduate of the University of North Carolina, Yoder was a Rhodes Scholar and received a degree in modern European political history and theory in 1958 from Oxford University. He joined the *Washington Star* as associate editor in 1975. Besides editorials, he writes a weekly opinion column. Yoder's ten editorials submitted for the Pulitzer covered an array of topics, including an antismoking crusade by the secretary of the U.S. Department of Health, Education and Welfare, the retirement of a U.S. senator and the visit to America of Israel's prime minister. The editorial included here, reacting to a speech by dissident Russian novelist Alexander Solzhenitsyn, is one that Yoder especially favors. The editorial is refreshing for its non-political subject matter and admirable for its depth of analysis. The most immediate criticism to be made of it regards the objectivity in Yoder's point of view. He implies Solzhenitsyn's understanding of American thought is restricted by his limited contact with—his distance from—American life. The other side of the coin, apparently unrecognized by Yoder, is that the editorial writer's understanding of American thought may be obscured by his closeness to the society. One might also question whether Yoder actually answers as many of Solzhenitsyn's charges as he presumes.

IT is probably a measure of their disquieting accuracy that Alexander Solzhenitsyn's periodic castigations of Western humanist values cry out for sharp rebuttal. He was back in the pulpit last week at the Harvard commencement; and the urge to respond sharply and defensively is, as usual, overpowering.

One's immediate instinct is to ask how much a Russian novelist living out his days behind a high fence, in an isolated Vermont village, really knows about the vibrant pluralistic society he finds so miserably deficient in spirituality. It is to recall that a cranky puritanism is the classic afflic- tion of great Russian men of letters; that few of them, with the exception of Turgenev, have ever been of ironic, tolerant or self-critical tempera- ment; that even Tolstoy, the greatest of all, ended his life in sour disgust with human variety and even with his own art, having concluded that all of it was vanity and frivolity.

Solzhenitsyn certainly needs placing in this tradition, for it explains quite a bit about his own jaundiced view of the world to which he came four years ago as an unwilling exile. Yet merely to establish the context of the matter is not to grapple responsibly with the matter itself.

What, to begin with, is he actually saying? The most familiar of his themes is, of course, that the liberal, skeptical pluralistic values of the West dangerously blind it to the relentlessness and evil of totalitarian ambitions—that we make fools of ourselves by attributing our own benevolent purposes to those who have very different ones. There is a disturbing truth in this; it is a worry that we must live with; but the remedy is never obvious. Is it not among the deadliest of many "totalitarian temptations" that free societies might adopt, in self-defense, the very character they set out to defend themselves against?

But politics and strategy are far from being the central feature of Mr. Solzhenitsyn's message. His prophecy isn't, in the strictest sense, political and in some respects is indeed anti-political. It belongs to other realms: historical, aesthetic, religious.

Historically, it is an attack on the fundamental shift of values which we traditionally associate with the Renaissance, in which the classical world's exalted estimate of the human personality was rediscovered and made the measure of things. Aesthetically, it is a keen and puritanical distaste for the frivolous and debased standards of popular culture—"TV stupor," as he calls it, and "intolerable music" and a pervasive commer- cialism that contaminates every purpose with a sales pitch of some kind. Religiously, it is the belief, quite pronounced in a sensitive Russian who has looked into the depths of the Stalinist hell, that the peoples of the West simply haven't suffered enough; that their dross is not sufficiently purged by misery.

These obsessions touch upon, but do not satisfactorily elaborate, complex truths about the West. They can't be dismissed with the mere protest that Mr. Solzhenitsyn dwells too much on the dark side and misses many concealed dimensions of seriousness—though that is also true.

In fact, in these highly subjective realms of perception, rebuttal as such is idle. There is no disputing spiritual perceptions, or tastes. Yet the great Russian prophet in our midst probably exaggerates Western decadence; and he certainly scants the complex value of free political and economic systems.

Such systems cannot, in their nature, refine or even predictably direct the tastes and moral purposes to which they give free play. Regimentation, for good or ill, is not their purpose. What Mr. Solzhenitsyn sees as spiritual chaos and vulgarity is the inescapable consequence of our view that the state is not, and cannot be, the appointed teacher of people. That is a role we reserve for private institutions—the church, the school, the family. It is their strengths or weaknesses that are reflected in the decay and confusion Mr. Solzhenitsyn deplores; it is to their strengthening that free peoples look for "spiritual" regeneration.

The West, says Mr. Solzhenitsyn, is not today an appealing model for the spiritual rebirth of the totalitarian nations. To which the right answer is: Of course it isn't—and can't be. Those who are regimented in an evil and soul-destroying system will not find an alternative model of regimentation by looking West.

They will find, however, a system that affords human nature the opportunity to declare itself freely, in all its glory and sordidness.